Introduction to Community Oral History

COMMUNITY ORAL HISTORY TOOLKIT

Nancy MacKay • Mary Kay Quinlan • Barbara W. Sommer

This five-volume boxed set is the definitive guide to all aspects of successfully conducting community projects that conform to best practices in the field of oral history. What are the fundamental principles that make one oral history project fly and another falter? The existing oral history methodology literature has traditionally focused on conducting academic research. In contrast, the *Toolkit* is specifically geared toward helping people develop and implement oral history projects in schools, service agencies, historical societies, community centers, churches, and other community settings. The five concise volumes, authored by leaders in the oral history field, offer down-to-earth advice on every step of the project, provide numerous examples of successful projects, and include forms that you can adapt to your specific needs. Together, these volumes are your "consultant in a box," offering the tools you need to successfully launch and complete your community oral history project.

Volume 1: *Introduction to Community Oral History*, by Mary Kay Quinlan with Nancy MacKay and Barbara W. Sommer

Volume 2: *Planning a Community Oral History Project*, by Barbara W. Sommer with Nancy MacKay and Mary Kay Quinlan

Volume 3: *Managing a Community Oral History Project*, by Barbara W. Sommer with Nancy MacKay and Mary Kay Quinlan

Volume 4: *Interviewing in Community Oral History*, by Mary Kay Quinlan with Nancy MacKay and Barbara W. Sommer

Volume 5: *After the Interview in Community Oral History*, by Nancy MacKay with Mary Kay Quinlan and Barbara W. Sommer

For additional information on this series, visit www.LCoastPress.com.

Community Oral History Toolkit

NANCY MACKAY • MARY KAY QUINLAN • BARBARA W. SOMMER

VOLUME 1

Introduction to Community Oral History

Mary Kay Quinlan
with **Nancy MacKay**
and **Barbara W. Sommer**

Left Coast
Press inc.

Walnut Creek, California

LEFT COAST PRESS, INC.
1630 North Main Street, #400
Walnut Creek, CA 94596

Left Coast
Press Inc.   www.LCoastPress.com

978-1-59874-241-5 Paperback
978-1-61132-689-5 eBook

Library of Congress Cataloging-in-Publication Data

MacKay, Nancy, 1945-
  Community oral history toolkit / Nancy MacKay, Mary Kay Quinlan, and Barbara W. Sommer
    5 v. ; cm.
  Includes bibliographical references and index.
  Contents: v. 1. Introduction to community oral history / by Mary Kay Quinlan with Nancy MacKay and Barbara W. Sommer -- v. 2. Planning a community oral history project / by Barbara W. Sommer, with Nancy MacKay and Mary Kay Quinlan -- v. 3. Managing a community oral history project / by Barbara W. Sommer with Nancy MacKay and Mary Kay Quinlan -- v. 4. Interviewing in community oral history / by Mary Kay Quinlan with Nancy MacKay and Barbara W. Sommer -- v. 5. After the interview in community oral history / by Nancy MacKay with Mary Kay Quinlan and Barbara W. Sommer.
  ISBN 978-1-59874-408-8 (complete set - pbk. : alk. paper) -- ISBN 978-1-61132-688-8 (complete set - consumer ebook) -- ISBN 978-1-61132-241-5 (volume 1 - pbk. : alk. paper) -- ISBN 978-1-61132-689-5 (volume 1 - consumer ebook) -- ISBN 978-1-61132-244-6 (volume 2 - pbk. : alk. paper) -- ISBN 978-1-61132-690-1 (volume 2 - consumer ebook) -- ISBN 978-1-61132-247-7 (volume 3 - pbk. : alk. paper) -- ISBN 978-1-61132-691-8 (volume 3 - consumer ebook) -- ISBN 978-1-61132-250-7 (volume 4 - pbk. : alk. paper) -- ISBN 978-1-61132-692-5 (volume 4 - consumer ebook) -- ISBN 978-1-61132-253-8 (volume 5 - pbk. : alk. paper) -- ISBN 978-1-61132-693-2 (volume 5 - consumer ebook)
  1. Oral history--Handbooks, manuals, etc. 2. Oral history--Methodology. 3. Interviewing--Handbooks, manuals, etc. 4. Local history--Methodology. I. Quinlan, Mary Kay. II. Sommer, Barbara W. III. Title.
  D16.14.M22 2012
  907.2--dc23
                    2012026513

Printed in the United States of America

Contents

Author's Preface | 7

Series Introduction | 9
Defining Oral History | 10
What You'll Find in the *Community Oral History Toolkit* | 11
Best Practices for Community Oral History Projects | 12
Toolkit Contents | 14

1 Understanding the Study of History | 17
What Historians Do | 18
How Oral History Has Evolved | 20
Oral History and Memory | 21
Accessibility of Oral History | 23

2 Defining Oral History, Defining Community | 25
Defining Oral History | 26
Defining Community | 28

3 Special Considerations for Community Oral History | 31
Insiders Versus Outsiders | 31
Working with Volunteers | 33
Challenging Collective Memories | 34
Finding Oral History Expertise | 36
Identifying a Repository | 37
Securing Project Funds | 38

4 **Community Oral History Tools and Technology | 39**

Technology Decisions | 39

Record-keeping Decisions | 42

5 **Preserving and Using Oral History Materials | 45**

Determining a Repository at the Outset | 46

Processing Oral History Materials | 47

Creating Secondary Products | 49

6 **Ethical Considerations for Oral Historians | 51**

Framing an Oral History Project | 52

Selecting Audio or Video Recording Equipment | 54

Choosing a Repository for Oral History Materials | 54

Securing Legal Release Agreements From Every Interviewee | 55

Obtaining Project Funding | 55

Documenting Historical Context | 56

7 **Exploring Best Practices for Community Oral History Projects | 59**

8 **Overview of the *Community Oral History Toolkit* | 67**

Appendix **Sample Forms for Managing Oral History Projects | 73**

Notes | 91

Glossary | 93

Resources | 107

Toolkit *Index* | 121

About the Authors 145

Author's Preface

What do you get when you combine three people in California, Minnesota, and Nebraska who have three different perspectives on oral history with a creative publisher and a really smart editor? You get this *Community Oral History Toolkit*. In these five volumes, we three coauthors, Barbara W. Sommer, Nancy MacKay, and myself, Mary Kay Quinlan, have pooled oral history expertise derived from our experiences as a public historian (Barbara), librarian (Nancy), and journalist (Mary Kay) and our passion for working with communities to create a set of handbooks for community oral historians to use in documenting and telling their communities' stories.

We have learned from some great teachers: the people who drew us into oral history in the first place; the oral historians we have met through our involvement with the Oral History Association, which is the national organization of oral history practitioners; the community oral historians we've worked with over the years; and those who graciously answered our questions and provided insights as we conducted research for these volumes. And we've learned a great deal from each other.

We started with the premise born of experience that many communities of all sorts want to use oral history techniques to document their history and explore their stories, but they often lack access to the oral history expertise that may reside in college and university libraries, history departments, and academic oral history centers. Sometimes community groups can tap into that expertise and infrastructure; other times they muddle along on their own, wanting to do the right thing to document and preserve their communities' histories but stumped to know just how to go about it.

Having worked with dozens of community groups of all sizes for many decades, we have attempted in these five volumes to distill the major lessons we have learned about how community oral historians can successfully navigate the oral history process of defining goals, making plans, doing research, conducting interviews, and assuring that those oral history interviews will be preserved for years to come. It's a process characterized by hard work and rich rewards—just as writing this *Community Oral History Toolkit* has been. For their enthusiasm and patience, we thank Mitch Allen and Stefania Van Dyke of Left Coast Press, Inc., our families and friends who endured our frustrations and celebrated our accomplishments, and the uncountable numbers of oral historians it has been our privilege to know and learn from over the years. Thank you all for making this project possible.

Mary Kay Quinlan

Series Introduction

Every community has them. The people who remember

- what happened when the church burned to the ground on Christmas Eve—how the congregation grieved, and then set aside its grief, got to work, and celebrated in a new sanctuary the next year;

- how strangers with pickup trucks took tornado victims to the nearest hospital when a record-breaking storm devastated the community;

- what it was like to bring a neighborhood together to fight the city's plans for a freeway; or

- how children, teachers, and community members felt the first day black and white youngsters shared the same classrooms in the aftermath of all the lawsuits attempting to block school integration.

Old newspaper clippings tell part of the story. So do public records that document the storm, the cost of neighborhood redevelopment, or the text of the court's decision. But what's often missing from the record is the *human* side of the issues, events, and ideas that we call history. And if you're reading the *Community Oral History Toolkit,* there's a good chance you already are thinking like an oral historian. You understand that it's important to add to the historical record first person information that can flesh out or reshape our understanding of past events.

Collectively, we three *Toolkit* authors have spent more than half a century working with community oral history projects, observing along the way how some succeed and others languish. You can readily find an excellent body of literature on oral history methodology, but it is designed for academic research and often does not translate well for unaffiliated community groups. So we've attempted in this five-volume *Toolkit* to identify some fundamental principles that lead to successful community oral history projects and to present practical tools and guidelines that we hope will be useful in a variety of community settings.

Defining Oral History

We define *community* broadly, using the definition found in the Oral History Association's pamphlet *Using Oral History in Community History Projects* (2010). The pamphlet defines community as any group of individuals bound together by a sense of shared identity. For the purposes of this *Toolkit*, we consider community oral history as that being undertaken by any group unaffiliated with an academic institution. Such groups could be neighborhood associations, historical societies, museums, libraries, professional associations, clubs, or any of the myriad ways people organize themselves to accomplish particular ends. Because we consider *community* in its broadest sense, we've included examples of community oral history projects that are diverse in size, topic of study, sponsoring organization, geographic location, and project goals. As you move through your own oral history project, and through the five *Toolkit* volumes, we encourage you to define your own community in the way that works best for you.

Community oral history projects differ in many ways from those originating in an academic setting. They usually

- lack institutional support for planning, managing, or funding;
- are organized around an exhibition, festival, performance, or publication;
- are driven by grant cycles and deadlines, sometimes with a specific goal determined by the funder;
- are carried out by volunteers or by a single paid staff member supervising volunteers;
- barter with local businesses or agencies for office space, technology expertise, and supplies;
- lack infrastructure, such as office space, storage, and computer equipment; and
- almost always have limited funds.

This *Toolkit* recognizes the special challenges community oral historians face and suggests ways to deal with them. It is predicated on the notion that a well-funded institutional setting is not a prerequisite to create solid oral history projects that will endure over time. What is required, however, is a fundamental understanding of oral history as a process that begins long before you ask the first interview question and ends long after you turn off the recorder.

For starters, here's how oral history is defined throughout these five volumes.

Oral history is primary source material collected in an interview setting with a witness to or a participant in an event or a way of life and is grounded in the context of time and place to give it meaning. It is recorded for the purpose of preserving the information and making it available to others. The term refers to both the process and the final product.

What You'll Find in the *Community Oral History Toolkit*

The *Community Oral History Toolkit* consists of five individual volumes. Each volume covers a particular aspect of doing oral history. Although each volume stands alone, the *Toolkit* is best seen as an integrated reference set, in much the same way that any particular aspect of doing oral history is dependent on decisions made at other stages of the process. The *Toolkit* is tightly organized, with subheadings, cross references within the text, and a comprehensive index for ready reference. You'll also find various visual elements, including hot spots (concise tips), definitions, sidebars (case studies and extended discussions), checklists, and figures that illustrate, elaborate, or draw attention to specific points. While all three of us have collaborated throughout the project, we divided the writing duties for the five volumes. Barbara Sommer is the lead author of Volumes 2 and 3; Mary Kay Quinlan is the lead author of Volumes 1 and 4; and Nancy MacKay is the lead author of Volume 5 and overall project coordinator, spearheading the research phase, marshaling the final details and keeping us all on task.

Volume 1. Introduction to Community Oral History. This volume sets the stage for your oral history project. It introduces the field to newcomers, with a discussion of the historical process, the evolution of oral history as an interdisciplinary research methodology, the nature of community and the nature of memory, and the legal and ethical underpinnings of oral history. And as such, Volume 1 importantly lays the theoretical groundwork for the practical application steps spelled out in detail in the subsequent volumes. It also introduces recording technology issues and options for oral history preservation, access, and use. Last, this volume elaborates on our Best Practices for Community Oral History Projects and presents a detailed overview of the remaining *Toolkit* volumes.

BEST PRACTICES
for Community Oral History Projects

1. **Familiarize yourself with the Oral History Association's guidelines.** First developed in 1968 and revised and updated regularly since then, these guidelines are the benchmark for the practice of ethical oral history and form the foundation on which solid oral history projects are built. Becoming familiar with them will help your project get off to a strong start.

2. **Focus on oral history as a process.** Keep in mind that, using standard historical research methods, you are setting out to explore a historical question through recorded interviews, giving it context and preserving it in the public record—in addition to whatever short-term goals your project may have such as using interview excerpts to create an exhibit or celebrate an anniversary.

3. **Cast a wide net to include community.** Make sure all appropriate community members are involved in your project and have an opportunity to make a contribution. Community members know and care the most about the project at hand, and the more closely they are involved in every aspect of it, the more successful it will be.

4. **Understand the ethical and legal ramifications of oral history.** Oral historians record deeply personal stories that become available in an archive for access both in the present and the future. So oral historians have ethical and legal responsibilities to abide by copyright laws and respect interviewees' wishes while also being true to the purposes of oral history.

Volume 2. Planning a Community Oral History Project. This volume walks you through all the planning steps needed to travel from an idea to a completed collection of oral history interviews. It will help you get started on firm ground, so you don't end up mired in quicksand halfway through your project or trapped in a maze of seemingly unsolvable problems.

Volume 3. Managing a Community Oral History Project. This volume takes the planning steps and puts them into action. It provides the practical details for turning your plans into reality and establishes the basis for guiding your project through the interviews and to a successful conclusion.

Volume 4. Interviewing in Community Oral History. The interview is the anchor of an oral history project. This volume guides the interviewer through all the steps from interview preparation to the follow-up. It includes tips on

5. **Make a plan.** At the outset, define your purpose, set goals, evaluate your progress, and establish record-keeping systems so details don't get out of control.

6. **Choose appropriate technology with an eye toward present and future needs.** Technology is necessary for recording interviews, preserving them in an archive, and providing access and using them for public displays. Make wise decisions about the technology you use.

7. **Train interviewers and other project participants to assure consistent quality.** Oral history interviews differ from some other interview-based research methods in the amount of background research and preparation required. Make sure interviewers and other personnel are thoroughly trained in oral history principles, interviewing techniques, recording technology, and ethics. The *Community Oral History Toolkit* covers all these topics.

8. **Conduct interviews that will stand the test of time.** This is the heart of the oral history process, but its success depends on laying solid groundwork.

9. **Process and archive all interview materials to preserve them for future use.** Oral history interviews and related materials should be preserved, cataloged, and made available for others to use in a suitable repository, such as a library, archive, or historical society.

10. **Take pride in your contribution to the historical record.** Share with the community what you've learned, and celebrate your success.

selecting interviewees, training interviewers, using recording equipment, and assessing ethical issues concerning the interviewer-interviewee relationship.

Volume 5. After the Interview in Community Oral History. Community projects often falter after the interviews are completed. This volume explains the importance of processing and archiving oral histories and takes readers through all the steps required for good archiving and for concluding an oral history project. It finishes with examples of creative ways community projects have used oral histories.

Finally, sample forms, checklists, and examples from the experiences of other community projects are provided that will help guide your project planning and a selected bibliography that will lead you to additional in-depth information on the various topics covered in the *Toolkit*.

We hope you will keep these volumes close at hand as you work step by step through your oral history project. Remember that the effort you put into doing the project right will pay off in unexpected ways far into the future. Many years from now you may well remember the exact words, tone of voice, or facial expression of an interviewee in answering questions only you thought to ask. And you may take satisfaction in knowing that your effort has preserved an important story—a piece of history that gives meaning to all our lives, both now and in the future.

Nancy MacKay, Mary Kay Quinlan, and Barbara W. Sommer

Toolkit Contents

Volume 1 **Introduction to Community Oral History**
    Author's Preface
    Series Introduction

    1. Understanding the Study of History
    2. Defining Oral History, Defining Community
    3. Special Considerations for Community Oral History
    4. Community Oral History Tools and Technology
    5. Preserving and Using Oral History Materials
    6. Ethical Considerations for Oral Historians
    7. Exploring Best Practices for Community Oral History Projects
    8. Overview of the *Community Oral History Toolkit*

    Appendix: Sample Forms for Managing Oral History Projects

    Notes
    Glossary
    Resources
    Toolkit *Index*
    About the Authors

Volume 2 **Planning a Community Oral History Project**
    Author's Preface
    Series Introduction

    1. Introduction
    2. Getting Started
    3. Project Design
    4. Planning for People and Infrastructure
    5. Equipment Planning
    6. All About Money

7. Winding Up

Appendix A: Planning Survey and Respondents

Appendix B: Equipment and Technology Terms

Appendix C: Recording Equipment Standards

Appendix D: Budget and Funding Terms

Notes
Further Reading
Index
About the Authors

Volume 3 **Managing a Community Oral History Project**

Author's Preface
Series Introduction

1. Introduction
2. The First Steps
3. People Management
4. Equipment Management
5. Money Management
6. Interview Management
7. Winding Up

Appendix: Management Survey and Respondents

Notes
Further Reading
Indcx
About the Authors

Volume 4 **Interviewing in Community Oral History**

Author's Preface
Series Introduction

1. What, Exactly, is an Oral History Interview?
2. Understanding the Ethics of Oral History Interviews
3. Before the Interview: What Project Teams Need to Do
4. Before the Interview: What Interviewers Need to Do
5. During the Interview
6. After the Interview

Notes
Further Reading
Index
About the Authors

Volume 5 **After the Interview in Community Oral History**

Author's Preface
Series Introduction

1. Getting Started
2. Processing
3. Transcribing
4. Cataloging
5. Preservation and Access
6. Winding Up
7. Using Oral Histories

Final Words

Appendix A: Fictitious Project Design Statement, *Project One—Volunteer*

Appendix B: Fictitious Project Design Statement, *Project Two—City*

Appendix C: Fictitious Project Design Statement, *Project Three—Historical Society*

Appendix D: Sample—Legal Release Agreement

Appendix E: Sample—Legal Release Agreement (Restrictions)

Appendix F: Sample Transcript Excerpt

Notes
Further Reading
Index
About the Authors

CHAPTER 1

Understanding the Study of History

Always there are stories. Hereditary griots in western Africa maintained their tribes' oral traditions generation after generation, telling the stories, reciting the poems, singing the songs. Aboriginal peoples in Australia etched their stories on the walls of caves, the symbolic art serving, perhaps, as memory aids. North American Plains Indians painted their stories—their histories—on buffalo hides in the form of winter counts, with one picture or symbol representing an important event marking each year. Family Bibles passed from one generation to the next listed births and deaths and, often, other landmark events in a family. Nineteenth century pioneers on the overland trails sometimes wept when they had to abandon family heirlooms in an attempt to lighten their loads as they headed toward the Continental Divide. They wept, in part because attached to those treasured objects were stories.

Stories that mattered.

Whether recited from memory through generations, painted stylistical-ly on rock walls or animal skins, or associated with keepsakes, stories from the past maintain traditions and often inform us how to live our lives.

But stories alone are not history. And collecting stories is not oral history. A critical component that sets oral history apart from merely collecting in-teresting, even compelling, stories is the reliance on a thoroughly researched, structured interview intended to elicit firsthand information about specific times, places, events, and ways of life. Oral historians seek to understand not only what happened, but also why things happened as they did. They ask follow-up questions to explore how people with firsthand knowledge of particular events made sense of them at the time and whether their under-standings have changed in the intervening years. Those elements contribute to the historical context of an oral history interview, and they often are miss-ing from the yarns told by even the most engaging storytellers.

What Historians Do

In an academic setting, historians strive to make sense of the past by reconstructing and interpreting past times and places by analyzing evidence that takes the form of official records, photographs, artifacts, and written documents of all sorts. We call those materials *primary sources,* because they were usually created by people who experienced the time, place, or event firsthand. Historians may then write books and scholarly articles presenting their analysis and interpretation of those primary sources. We call such writings *secondary sources.* Students and other historians customarily use these resources to pursue further research.

For the historian, finding primary sources can be like going on a treasure hunt, looking for clues in

- letters
- diaries, journals, and personal memoirs
- calendars or date books
- photographs, slides or movies
- maps
- statistics
- survey results
- physical artifacts of all sorts
- recordings of speeches
- land records
- tax rolls
- minutes of meetings
- high school yearbooks, and
- records kept by government agencies at the federal, state, or local level.

All such items, and a multitude of other examples, may be found in museums, libraries, universities, government agencies, and other public repositories. Together they constitute what we call the historical record.

Oral historians add to that historical record when they create oral history interviews. The interviews themselves are primary documents that become part of the storehouse of information available for academic historians, public historians, and anyone else to use. Indeed, people interested in many scholarly fields, not just history, use oral history research methods, from gerontologists seeking to learn more about elders' experiences to public lands managers seeking information about traditional uses of protected wilderness areas. Whenever their interviews are archived in a public repository, that information, too, becomes part of the historical record for all.

Despite the enormous volume of primary and secondary documents available for historians—and communities, families, and individuals—to make sense of the past, the historical record is inevitably incomplete. Documents may be lost or damaged in a flood or fire or by hungry mice. Or they may be hidden in a musty attic or damp basement, long forgotten by those who created them and set them aside for safekeeping. Or they may simply fade with time so they are no longer legible, hiding the historical secrets once inscribed there. Or they may conceal more than they reveal, a phenomenon easily understood by anyone who has ever been a member or secretary of a civic organization. Rare are the minutes of such organizations' meetings that don't gloss over a bitter argument by saying something like, "A lively discussion ensued."

One of the challenges in dealing with all such historical tidbits is trying to understand the context in which they were created. Doing so often requires digging into alternate primary sources to shed more light on situations or events, as in the case of meeting minutes designed to mask controversy. Contemporary newspaper accounts, correspondence among the various players, and municipal records such as property ownership, tax records, and zoning permits all can add details. And oral history interviews can be one more tool for piecing together a fuller understanding of past times and places.

But sometimes, the context of historical documents remains elusive. Diaries of women who crossed the North American continent in the nineteenth[th] century, for example, can offer tantalizing clues to life on the overland trails.[1] But modern readers cannot help but wonder about the women who jotted down their observations, sometimes at length, in the diaries and letters that have survived. Were they writing to deal with their own emotions? To create a record for their children? To gild their experiences so as to induce family members back East to join them? Did those women write more when the day had been particularly strenuous? Or write less? Or not at all? Historians who have studied such writings have pieced together, collectively, some sense of what the overland trail experience was like, but the historical context of the documents themselves is often inadequate.

Moreover, the artifacts and documents that comprise the historical record reflect the biases and the world view of those who created them, making absolute objectivity impossible. Even something as apparently straightforward as mapmaking involves human decisions: How large does a village or settlement or cluster of dwellings have to be to appear on the map?

If a creek or stream is known by more than one name, what will it be called on the map? And who gets to decide?

The ancient Greek historian Thucydides recognized this inherent subjectivity of historical sources. Thucydides is widely considered the father of modern historical methods, because he gathered firsthand testimony in writing his accounts of the Peloponnesian wars between Sparta and Athens in the fifth century B.C. He observed that eye witnesses gave different accounts of the same events and suggested that was because they favored one side or the other or, perhaps, because memory isn't perfect. More than two millennia later, contemporary oral historians are wise to remember Thucydides' observations.

How Oral History Has Evolved

Long before Thucydides' day, and continuing to modern times, communities have transmitted their culture through word of mouth in the form of stories, songs, myths, epic poems and the like entrusted from one generation to the next. In this sense, history has always been oral.

More recently, beginning in the late nineteenth[th] and early twentieth[th] centuries, the practice of conducting interviews with participants in historically important events began to catch on in the United States as a method of conducting historical research. Scholar Hubert Howe Bancroft based his seven-volume *History of California*, published between 1884 and 1890, largely on interviews. In the 1930s, the Depression-era Federal Writer's Project conducted interviews with former slaves. On June 6, 1944, a young Army sergeant named Forrest Pogue, stationed on a hospital ship off Normandy Beach, used a then-new technology called a wire recorder to interview wounded soldiers evacuated from Normandy on D-Day. He went ashore two days later and continued recording interviews in what was the beginning of a process that ultimately led to the establishment of structured oral history programs in the armed forces and in major academic research centers.

In 1948, Columbia University launched its Oral History Research Office, later renamed the Columbia Center for Oral History. Similar scholarly research centers followed at the University of California, Berkeley in 1954 and at the University of California Los Angeles in 1958, thus securing a respected place for oral history in academia.

The early focus of many oral history programs was on documenting the lives and times of leading political and other public figures. A 50th anniversary compact disc containing excerpts from Columbia University's collection of thousands of interviews includes Thurgood Marshall, Fred Astaire, Dorothy

Parker and Orvil Faubus as interviewees, among more than a dozen others.[2] Many of the presidential libraries contain extensive collections of oral history interviews with presidential advisers, contemporary office holders, and behind-the-scenes personnel who played roles in the presidents' administrations.

By the 1970s, growing interest in social history and rapid changes in recording technology that made cassette tape recorders widely available took oral history back to its early roots, as reflected in Pogue's interviews with ordinary soldiers, not just generals. The run-up to the U.S. Bicentennial celebration in 1976 sparked interest by families and communities in exploring their pasts and further solidified the role of oral history methods in documenting the lives of everyday people, a practice that became known as "history from the ground up," in contrast with a "top down" view of understanding the past. From that perspective, oral history became an important research technique in emerging scholarly fields of women's studies and ethnic studies and found a place in many college classrooms. Even elementary and secondary school teachers began to employ oral history activities, as their classes studied family and community history.

In recent years, the digital revolution has continued to bring simple recording equipment—both audio and video—well within the reach of many. And it has also vastly enlarged the options for sharing recorded interviews through publication on the World Wide Web. That, in turn, has raised new questions about interview transcription, preservation, and copyright protection, among other management issues. But it also has contributed to vast stores of oral history interviews in video, audio, and transcripts being available online.

Oral History and Memory

Just as the evolution of recording technology has changed the practice of oral history and made it readily accessible to grass roots organizations, so also have the theoretical underpinnings of the field evolved, particularly in exploring the nature of memory.[3]

Human variability makes the study of memory a complex scientific field, attracting the attention of neuroscientists, psychologists, sociologists, psycholinguists, gerontologists, human development experts and others. They study everything from slugs and fruit flies to human infants and adults to tease out greater knowledge about how memory works. To cite one example, for more than a century researchers in the field of psychology and the law have explored aspects of eyewitness memory.[4] Their work has established that memories are malleable, influenced by what happens to a person after an event as well as by receiving new information that can cause people to reconstruct their memories. Moreover, the advent of neuroimaging devices that make it possible for scientists to observe electrical activity in different parts of the brain during psychological experiments has demonstrated that memory is a much more complex phenomenon than was once believed. The human brain is not like a computer that stores bits of information, keeping them available for recall in the same way a Google search coughs up facts. Indeed, for oral historians, what often matters more than an interviewee's ability to recall specific, discrete facts is how interviewees use memories of the past to make sense of their worlds. It is, in fact, the human ability to be retrospective and reinterpret previous experiences that makes oral history a living window into the past.[5]

While memory research focuses on many different aspects of the subject, oral historians may be most interested in conclusions historian Valerie Raleigh Yow has drawn from extensive review of the literature reported in her *Recording Oral History: A Guide for the Humanities and Social Sciences*. According to Yow, memory researchers have found that, in general:

- People's memories of the basic information about an event will persist, even if they forget some of the details.

- People recall firsthand information about events that they were part of better than they can remember secondhand information.

- People tend to remember events that involved a high level of mental or emotional involvement.[6]

People who have been in the same place at the same time will have different memories of an event because they experience it within their own frame of reference and accumulated life experience. Oral historians work with what our brains have encoded and filtered into our memories through our belief systems, culture, personalities, gender, and daily lives. Information stored in memory and collected in an oral history interview gives us access to an interviewee's unique, first-person interpretation of the past. That means oral historians will unearth different understandings and interpretations of the same events, just as Thucydides did. Exploring those differences—and similarities—in perspective is what enables an oral historian to go beyond the superficial facts and draw a more nuanced, deeper understanding of the time and place in question.

Oral historians also deal with the phenomenon of collective memory, in which individuals' memories of past times and places are influenced by public discourse about events in a community and by news and entertainment media portrayals. The challenge for oral historians is to go beyond those expressions

Lessons From Class Reunions

Scholars' conclusions about the individual, subjective, and malleable nature of memory come as no surprise to anyone who has attended a class reunion, where memories of particular events that loomed large when everyone was in high school may take on an entirely different cast many years later. And some of the classmates likely have forgotten these events altogether.

of collective memory—the public stories that *everyone* supposedly believes—to unearth deeper layers of understanding about the past. Exploring—and challenging—collective memory can be particularly tricky for community oral historians and is discussed in detail in Chapter 3.

Memory researchers also have explored how people reinterpret their experiences in light of new experiences or events, a phenomenon at the root of the phrase "I changed my mind." New information or a new perspective can make people view past experiences in a different light; an occurrence that seemed life-altering when it happened may have proved to be much less significant in hindsight. Exploring such reinterpretations can be a rich line of questioning for oral historians.

Accessibility of Oral History

The enthusiasm and energy with which everyday people and groups turn to oral history as a way to understand and document their pasts have contributed new vibrancy to the field. The digital revolution has created new ways to publish oral history materials and new ways to examine interview content. And the oral history process itself is readily accessible to those who want to learn how to use it. As a result, teachers, urban planners, gerontologists, filmmakers, scientists, environmentalists, ethnic neighborhood activists, musicians, veterans groups, factory workers, and all manner of other groups have adopted oral history techniques to reach their particular goals, whether documenting a particular event, exploring a neglected community's perspective, or celebrating milestones. This *Community Oral History Toolkit* aims to assist such groups in their efforts.

CHAPTER 2

Defining Oral History, Defining Community

Oral transmission of cultural information is an ancient practice that covers a diverse array of data—origin stories, where to hunt, why family intermarriage is taboo—as well as an array of forms in which culturally and historically important information is conveyed—stories told only in winter, songs sung on particular occasions, epic poems ritually performed.

Families, too, transmit culturally important information in much the same way. Grandpa recalls the same story every Christmas about his mother singing "Stille Nacht" in the German she learned as a child. Mother tells the urban-reared grandchildren what it was like to grow up on a farm. Perhaps your family hands down stories about emigrating to the United States from Ireland, Germany or one of the Scandinavian countries during the great waves of 19th century immigration. Or maybe your stories recall ancestors from China who built the railroad across America. Perhaps your family was part of the great migration of slave descendants who made the move from the Old South to the industrial cities of the North. Or maybe your family's stories recount a hand-to-mouth existence as migratory fieldworkers up and down the length of California. Or perhaps your family has a more recent tale of fleeing Somalia to a refugee camp in Ethiopia before arriving in the United States.

Such oral transmissions of family history, repeated from one generation to the next, often provide rich, if sometimes apocryphal, details that help people define themselves in relation to others and often set forth a moral code to live by.

Defining Oral History

But none of this is oral history as we use the term throughout the *Community Oral History Toolkit*. In a generic sense, the term *oral history* has become a popular, if informal, brand applied to many settings in which people talk about the past. To avoid confusion with such casual use of the term, the following definition has been used throughout the *Community Oral History Toolkit*:

Oral history is primary source material collected in an interview setting with a witness to or a participant in an event or a way of life and is grounded in context of time and place to give it meaning. It is recorded for the purpose of preserving the information and making it available to others. The term refers to both the process and the final product.

With this definition as a standard, the *Toolkit* sets forth a process by which to embark on an oral history project leading to a collection of interviews that will stand the test of time. Consider each of the elements in this definition. An oral history interview:

- creates a new primary source of information, just as diaries, public meeting minutes, and physical artifacts are primary sources;
- relies on a structured interview, not a casual recitation of memories;
- elicits firsthand information from someone in a position to describe a particular time, place, or event;
- is grounded in research about the particular time, place, or event, enabling the interviewer to ask questions establishing context and seeking depth and detail;
- is recorded at a level of quality that can be preserved; and
- is made available to others in any of a variety of means, respecting appropriate ethical and legal practices.

Other research methods that rely on asking questions share some characteristics with oral history, but it's important to keep in mind some critical differences that set oral history apart. For example, sociologists or political scientists who are engaged in survey research frequently rely on asking questions of their research subjects. But a sociologist usually follows a prescribed script, asking questions in precisely the same order and in the same way, and is less likely to allow interviewees to offer open-ended responses of their own choosing. Or the questions might be on a printed or online questionnaire with no leeway for individual responses that differ from the predetermined

Oral history refers to both the process and the final product.

choices. Moreover, interviewee anonymity is usually a key element of interview-based research conducted in social science fields, which is the complete opposite of an oral history project in which interviewees are identified by name and biographical information about them is an important part of providing interview context.

Folklorists often conduct interviews, much as oral historians do, and indeed there can be significant overlap. But folklorists may focus largely on collecting traditional songs, stories, poems, or other community traditions passed down through generations. As a result, the people a folklorist records singing or performing traditional music, for example, are not the individuals who wrote the songs in the first place. Oral historians, on the other hand, focus on collecting firsthand information from interviewees who themselves experienced particular events or ways of life.

Genealogists conducting family research also may conduct interviews with extended family members to fill out the details of their ancestors' lives. In so doing, they may ask elderly relatives to recall aspects of their early lives or the lives of others they knew. Sometimes such interviews may be recorded. Other times, the elderly family member may be asked to write down her memories, or the genealogist may take notes and write up the information to share with the rest of the family. But these kinds of question-based information-gathering techniques also differ from oral history in several ways. The interviews may not be based on a structured, focused interview, but may simply take the form of asking Great-Aunt Mabel to share her memories of times gone by. Moreover, genealogists are less likely to record such interviews at a quality necessary for long-term preservation. And it is unlikely the material will be archived and accessible for general public use.

Journalists routinely record interviews with people about firsthand experiences, and sometimes such interviews have been carefully researched and structured. But what journalists do also differs from what oral historians do in several important ways. Reporters conducting interviews almost always have specific, short-term purposes for using the information in newspaper or online stories or broadcast news or documentary projects. Sometimes journalists record interviews for their own reference and do not use equipment that creates recordings suitable for broadcast or online use, much less long-term preservation. And even when recordings are made with broadcast-quality equipment, journalists are highly unlikely to donate their interviews to a repository that will make them available to others. To be sure, community oral historians often have specific plans to use portions of their interviews in some kind of public setting or publication in the reasonably near future, particularly if a project is sparked by the idea of contributing oral history information to an anniversary celebration. But journalists are often working on a much tighter schedule for creating an immediate story or newscast and generally have little interest in future possible uses of their materials or in long-term preservation and access, both of which are critical characteristics of oral history projects.

Defining Community

While the *Community Oral History Toolkit* uses a specific definition of oral history that may be narrower than the casual use of the term, its definition of community may be seen as quite broad. In the most general sense, a community is a group of people with something in common. The Oral History Association pamphlet *Using Oral History in Community History Projects* offers a more detailed definition: "The term community encompasses nearly every kind of human group conceivable, from a family to political, cultural, occupational, or religious organizations whose membership is far-flung. Whatever its size or constituency, a community consists of individuals bound together by a sense of shared identity."[7] For purposes of the *Community Oral History Toolkit,* the "sense of shared identity" is augmented by adding this caveat: The intent is to serve oral history projects generally unaffiliated with a university or other academic institution.

 A community is a group of people sharing a sense of identity.

Here's an example of a community oral history project that illustrates the definition of community as people sharing a sense of identity. In 1981, interviewers from several local historical organizations in Minnesota developed an oral history project that aimed to document the work in Minnesota of the Civilian Conservation Corps (CCC), a New Deal work-relief program for young men.[8] The project tapped into a strong and vibrant community of CCC alumni. Community members supported the project and participated in it with great pride. They understood its importance in collecting memories about a difficult time in the nation's history and their roles in it. The resulting oral histories open a window onto the daily lives of CCC enrollees, describing their work in Minnesota on what is now called the greatest conservation program in American history. And the thousands of photographs, documents, and artifacts donated through the project helped build a public archive and a museum dedicated to the Minnesota CCC.

The CCC enrollees constitute a community of memory, a group with a shared sense of identity. They came from different backgrounds, had many different life experiences, and lived in scattered locations. But it was the months or years they spent in the CCC that brought them together as a community of memory.

Communities of memory share a common knowledge base but are not necessarily homogeneous. Indeed, community oral history projects aim to include people who represent all sides of the project topic. To use the Civilian Conservation Corps as an example, the majority of people involved in the CCC were enrollees, called "boys," the predominantly white 18-to-25-year-olds who were unemployed and whose families were eligible for relief. But they are not the only people in the CCC community of memory. CCC camps were run by regular or reserve Army officers. CCC conservation work programs were directed and managed by state or federal conservation personnel, including foresters, park directors, and soil conservation employees. Work program directors hired local men with specific skills to teach and work with enrollees. Camps had education programs, often run by unemployed teachers. Architects and engineers designed the buildings and structures enrollees built. African-American enrollees served both in segregated companies and, for a time in some northern states, in integrated companies. All-black companies often had white commanders and black non-commissioned officers. The federal Bureau of Indian Affairs organized the CCC-Indian Division, a parallel program that served enrolled tribal members in work programs directed by Indians and non-Indians. All of these people are part of the CCC community of memory.

Your community of memory will be the people with information and a sense of shared identity in the community whose history you seek to document. Your interviewees may come from a variety of backgrounds, just as the CCC interviewees did. They will represent many sides or parts of your project topic, and they may represent divergent or opposing views. But with their shared sense of identity, they will all be members of your community of memory and their participation will enrich your oral history project.

Although the CCC project illustrates a large community of memory, oral history projects can be quite the opposite. For example, Arapahoe County, Colorado, which encompasses Denver's southern and eastern suburbs, was historically a politically conservative, Republican county. But that changed in 2008 when Democratic presidential candidate Barack Obama fired up volunteers, many of whom had not previously been politically active, to work for his campaign in what became a pivotal county on Election Day.[9] One of those volunteers, Steve Kennedy, offered his home as a staging area for political canvassing and was struck by the stories he kept hearing: about why people had been motivated to devote their shoe leather to Obama; about the experience of walking neighborhoods, knocking on doors; about the people who opened those doors. Steve knew that his friend Cyns Nelson had oral-history expertise from her work at the Boulder Carnegie Library for Local History, so he called Cyns and told her: "Something important is happening here." Thus an oral history project was born.

Cyns and Steve concluded that the stories behind the remarkable out-pouring for a Democratic presidential candidate in a historically Republican area merited capturing and saving, even if no immediate use for the material was in sight. They developed a legal release agreement and a focused list of themes to pursue, samples of which can be found in **Volume 4** of the *Toolkit*. About a hundred people initially expressed interest in being interviewees, and eventually twenty-nine of them were interviewed by the following spring.

The interviews revealed a remarkable depth of emotion among the campaign volunteers and compelling stories about their involvement. One became tearful over recalling how he registered a woman to vote.

I could see that she took it very, very seriously. [Pause.] You could feel the weight…. She says, "In 35 years I've never voted; this will be the first time." And you know…. At the time I had such a hard time holding back the tears, 'cause it felt SO good. It felt so good.

Another volunteer talked about his abiding fear of what would happen to the country if Republican John McCain were elected but couldn't serve out his term, catapulting vice presidential candidate Sarah Palin into the White House. Many interviewees repeatedly used the word "empowered" to describe how they felt about campaigning, and said they realized they had been isolated from their neighbors and hadn't realized how demographically diverse their neighborhoods had become. One woman said, "All of a sudden we were talking to people and realized we were a community."

Again, while the interviewees in this project were limited to those who shared the experience of campaigning for Barack Obama, the documented experience was one of discovering a larger, physical community. With recordings made when things were fresh in people's minds, a community of memory has now been preserved.

CHAPTER 3

Special Considerations for Community Oral History

Community groups unaffiliated with a university or other academic institution face all the same challenges anyone faces in embarking on an oral history project: making a plan, finding workers, researching the topic, identifying people to interview, conducting interviews, and processing them for archival preservation. The *Community Oral History Toolkit* provides complete information in the remaining four volumes to help you accomplish all those tasks.

But community oral history projects also may face some additional challenges. They often have to:

- address insider versus outsider issues,

- deal with the vagaries of volunteers,

- overcome hurdles related to prevailing collective memories,

- struggle to find oral history expertise

- identify an appropriate repository, and

- secure funding for the project.

This chapter introduces these additional tasks, providing insights on some of the rewards and pitfalls you may encounter.

Insiders Versus Outsiders

To a certain extent, most oral history projects have to address issues related to how closely project planners and staff are tied to the individuals they intend to interview. Students in university history classes, for example, often are tasked with conducting oral history interviews as part of ongoing projects. Perhaps they're part of a project designed to document the history of an inner-city neighborhood. In such a case, the students are unlikely to be familiar with the neighborhood or its residents, which means they will have to make special efforts to establish credibility with the people they interview. This lack of understanding can be one of the disadvantages of being an outsider, particularly if one is associated with a college or university. College students assigned to an oral history project may be perceived by their interviewees as transients without any real interest in or commitment to the project other than earning a grade. Such a perception, of course, might be inaccurate, but it nonetheless can affect the way potential interviewees react, making them cautious about participating in oral history interviews conducted by people they don't know and aren't sure whether they can trust.

On the other hand, outsiders often have a significant advantage over insiders, or people closely connected to the community or subject at hand, as they tend to approach the subject with a more open mind and have fewer preconceived notions about what they'll discover. Outsiders tend to be more willing to engage in wide-ranging research in preparing for interviews and less likely to make assumptions about who should be interviewed and what themes should be explored. In addition, they can bring a fresh perspective to a subject simply because they have little previous knowledge about the particular time, place, or individuals involved.

In contrast, people involved in community oral history projects tend to be the ultimate insiders. They get involved in a community oral history project because they are passionate about documenting some aspect of the community's history. Often that means that they, themselves, have been players in that history. As a result, they may have a great deal of firsthand information about the subject at hand, which may give them a deeper understanding of the issues to be explored. They also are likely to know many of the individuals who should be interviewed to shed light on those issues. And as interviewers, they are presumed to have credibility when asking questions, because they have a storehouse of knowledge that an outsider wouldn't have.

But there's a downside. Sometimes insiders can be *too* close to the subject. They may have to consciously stand back and take a broader view of the topic at hand, and they may have to play devil's advocate when exploring controversial matters. In short, they have to be willing to adopt the perspective of an outsider to research the issues and ask probing questions, even if they think they already know the answers. In other words, they have to be willing to discover something new.

Community oral history projects can face yet another wrinkle in the insider-outsider arena. In seeking to attract many participants in a project, community groups may attract newcomers who want to be involved, even though they may lack the fuller storehouse of knowledge longtime participants in the community may have. Thus the management challenge may be to incorporate the strengths and minimize the weaknesses of both kinds of participants. Insiders and outsiders both can play effective roles in a community oral history project, whether as interviewers, interviewees, or support staff. But it's important for everyone to realize the particular skills and knowledge base they have, be willing to learn from each other, and contribute accordingly.

Working With Volunteers

The nineteeth[th] century French aristocrat Alexis de Tocqueville described with amazement in his classic *Democracy in America* the propensity of Americans to form associations and to volunteer to do, well, almost anything. First published in English in 1840, *Democracy in America* reported his observation:

> *Americans of all ages, all conditions, and all dispositions, constantly form associations. They have not only commercial and manufacturing companies, in which all take part, but associations of a thousand other kinds—religious, moral, serious, futile, extensive or restricted, enormous or diminutive…. I have often admired the extreme skill with which the inhabitants of the United States succeed in proposing a common object to the exertions of a great many men, and in getting them voluntarily to pursue it.*[10]

It has been nearly 200 years since Alexis de Tocqueville made those observations, and in many important ways, nothing has changed. Community groups undertaking an oral history project readily understand they will be relying on volunteers to make things happen. Community oral history projects may sometimes be able to pay a project director or coordinator, but the project tasks usually are carried out by volunteers who donate their time and energy.

Volunteers, of course, can be wonderful. They are enthusiastic, creative, and goal driven. They network in the community to round up needed resources. They help each other solve problems. Their community connections provide links to potential interviewees. They work countless hours without pay, save for pizza and soft drinks at the end of the day.

As with most wonderful things, however, there's a flip side to working with volunteers. They can be single-minded or capricious. They can be argumentative, seeking constantly to change a project's direction. They can be unreliable. They can lose interest and drift away. Their kids can get sick or their elderly parents can need extra help. They can lose their job or get a new one that takes up more time.

Volunteers, in short, will make—or break—a community oral history project. So here's the key to success in volunteer-run projects: pull together a varied pool of interested people with disparate skills and find tasks for everyone that match their skills. Volunteer community groups generally are quite good at this. Community members know who can be counted on to come through and meet a deadline. They know who can come through if she has a little help. They know who will promise to take on a task but who never seems to get the job done. And they know how to keep that person involved, at least tangentially, so he'll continue to feel that he's part of the process.

The need to make effective use of volunteers for an oral history project is one of the reasons it's important to provide appropriate training for them. Community oral history projects are unlikely to recruit a large corps of volunteers who are already experienced oral historians. So it's important to make sure volunteers have the training they need to conduct skillful interviews, including training on using recording devices. Everyone is not suited to being an oral history interviewer, but without appropriate training opportunities even the most capable volunteers will be less likely to succeed.

Community oral history projects tend to have a core leadership group that spearheads the planning and keeps things going. If the project leaders understand the planning and management functions an oral history project requires, they will be able to match the skills of volunteers with the tasks at hand. The remaining volumes of the *Community Oral History Toolkit* spell out in detail the tasks that need to be accomplished, which should help project leaders get off to a good start with their volunteers.

Plus, it always helps to say thank you and take turns ordering pizza.

Challenging Collective Memories

In the modern era of instant communications, it doesn't take long for a prevailing narrative to emerge in the wake of major breaking news events.

- Within days of a cruise ship running aground off the Italian coast early in 2012, the captain who abandoned ship was widely lampooned as a "chicken of the sea."

- Before the dust settled at the World Trade Center, the Pentagon and a field near Shanksville, Pennsylvania, on Sept. 11, 2001, the tragedy took on a storyline of Muslim extremists versus innocent, heroic Americans.

- When the so-called housing bubble burst in 2007, leaving countless homeowners with mortgages of more than their houses were worth, the public narrative put all the blame on Wall Street shenanigans.

- When over-leveraged Midwestern farmers faced falling land values and commodity prices in the mid-1980s, the prevailing public theme was of farmers as victims, and stories focused on family violence and suicide in the agricultural heartland.

Such public narratives or storylines often become the collective memory of an event, even though they almost always are oversimplified at best and at worst can be just plain wrong. But the public narrative often prevails. It may be because players who could recount a different version of the events remain hidden from view. Or it may be that news editors are quick to move on to the next big story. Or perhaps it's because we have limited attention spans and an oversimplified tale is all we can absorb. Or maybe the truth would be too hard to accept. Or perhaps the situation in question gives rise to multiple story lines, all of them true. In such cases, oral history projects can document those multiple, perhaps conflicting, views, which in turn often contribute to a more complex, nuanced understanding of the past.

In the case of the economic turmoil in agriculture in the 1980s, one interviewing project for a doctoral dissertation uncovered quite a different tale from the prevailing farmer-as-victim storyline.[11] Many Midwestern farmers had borrowed heavily to expand their operations to meet rising export demand in the 1970s. Soaring inflation rates made land a good investment. But conditions changed abruptly in the early 1980s, when worldwide crop production increased and sharp changes in the value of the dollar overseas dried up export demand. Inflation came to a halt, land values plummeted, and credit for farmers evaporated. Both the popular and scholarly press portrayed farmers as victims facing hard times through no fault of their own. But far from seeing themselves as pawns in an international marketplace over which they had no control, farmers in a community study in Nebraska openly took responsibility for unwise borrowing decisions. One interviewee said:

> Some people blame somebody because they don't want to blame themselves. But it's nobody's fault but our own…. We went out and bought. We just kept buying, because everything was going up. You could buy a piece of ground for $500 an acre and two years later it was worth $700, two years later it was worth $1,000…. We made a mistake and we admit it. I'm not ashamed to admit it.[12]

Community oral history projects may have to contend with this phenomenon of hidden memories that don't match the prevailing storyline and be prepared to challenge the community's collective memory if the research and interviews suggest alternative versions of the past. But it might not be easy.

Oral history explores alternative explanations of the past.

Just as some families have skeletons in their closets that no one is willing to dust off and confront, so also might communities prefer to leave aspects of their pasts unexamined. But the beauty of oral history is that it creates a platform for exploring alternative explanations of the past, without passing judgment on interviewees' memories. Embarking on a community oral history project with that frame of reference gives a community the freedom to explore all aspects of an unexamined past—the prevailing collective memory as well as the hidden ones no one has been willing to hear until your project committed to explore them.

A community oral history project that commits at the outset to casting a wide net with the aim of documenting all sides of an issue will have a built-in advantage in challenging prevailing collective memories. If people with disparate perspectives are involved in planning the project, it might be easier to find and document information that previously received scant attention. When multiple, conflicting story lines emerge, however, people involved in community oral history projects should resist the temptation to attempt to determine once and for all which side is right. The Nebraska farmers who were willing to take responsibility for their own financial crises, for example, merely illustrate that the prevailing farmer-as-victim view was an oversimplified, one-dimensional perspective. And history is seldom simple.

Finding Oral History Expertise

Oral history projects based in academic institutions generally have ready access to historians, librarians, and archivists who can guide project participants. Unaffiliated community groups, on the other hand, may struggle to find the oral history expertise they need.

If you're reading this volume of the *Community Oral History Toolkit*, you've already started to solve that problem. In addition to the detailed instructions throughout the *Toolkit* addressing every phase of an oral history project, you'll find an extensive list of resources—books, articles, websites and the like—that will allow you to delve more deeply into themes the *Toolkit* volumes explore. You'll also find examples of successful community oral history projects and perhaps be inspired by the public presentations that grew out of their efforts.

In addition to using the *Community Oral History Toolkit* as your guide, you also should join the Oral History Association, which is the major national organization of oral historians, and the H-Oralhist listserv, as well as any local or regional oral history groups. National, regional or local groups often sponsor training workshops for beginners as well as for people well versed in oral history techniques. The listserv offers another way to network with people who may be able to provide answers to problems your project has encountered.

State humanities councils and state historical societies also can be useful sources of information and, sometimes, funding for community oral history efforts. Faculty members at area colleges and universities and staff at nearby state or national historic sites also might be resources, if they are knowledgeable about oral history techniques.

Above all, don't hesitate to ferret out other community groups—in your area or across the country—that have embarked on oral history projects. They tend to be extraordinarily willing to share what they learned, will steer you away from pitfalls they encountered, and will cheer your successes.

Identifying a Repository

Because oral histories are meant to be preserved and made available to others, community groups that embark on an oral history project are well advised to identify a library, museum, archives, or other such entity that can become the permanent home of the materials your project will generate. Projects that grow out of academic institutions, by contrast, generally have a built-in home for the oral history materials they generate. For community projects, finding a home for the oral histories and associated materials is a task best tackled at the outset, as the ultimate disposition of the materials might have a bearing on what equipment you choose to record the interviews and the legal release agreements you ask participants to sign. **Volume 2,** *Planning a Community Oral History Project,* and **Volume 5,** *After the Interview in Community Oral History,* provide detailed information about dealing with repositories.

The individuals and institutions you encounter in your quest for oral history expertise also may prove helpful in identifying a permanent repository. Indeed, local or state historical societies or public libraries may be willing to accept your oral history collection, as well as providing informal advice, equipment loans, or more formal consulting services. Or perhaps your community oral history project focuses on a subject of interest to a state or national association that maintains archives pertaining to its area of expertise. Or, even though your project isn't the brainchild of an academic institution, some college or university archives might take your materials as part of their special collections, under certain circumstances. The bottom line? It never hurts to ask.

Securing Project Funds

Even the smallest community oral history projects operated entirely by volunteers have expenses. Although those expenses may not require cash, it's important to recognize the value of the time the volunteers put in and the value of the in-kind contributions people make when they lend recording equipment and a computer or pay out-of-pocket for postage and copy paper or the gas to drive their own car to an interviewee's home.

When the scope of a community oral history project outstrips its capability to be self-funded, assessing available options is an important part of project planning; this step is detailed in **Volume 2,** *Planning a Community Oral History Project.* There's no need to resort to bake sales and car washes until you've thoroughly explored other possibilities.

- Local schools, community colleges, museums, and libraries can be sources from which you could borrow audio-visual equipment that would meet your needs.

- Area businesses might be willing to donate supplies and a computer or other office equipment.

- Local community foundations or state humanities councils can be sources of grants for which you could apply. One of your project volunteers might have grant-writing experience you could draw on in seeking such support.

- Businesses and organizations whose interests relate to the focus of your project could be approached for cash or in-kind assistance.

Whatever combination of financial resources a community oral history project relies on, it's important to have a clear sense at the outset of how much the project is going to cost. Developing this estimate can be an exacting challenge for groups without a preexisting infrastructure, but a willingness to address budgetary issues from the beginning, and develop realistic plans, will help prevent disappointment later on, should the lack of funds force an early end to the project.

Your community oral history project will increase its chances of success if it anticipates these special considerations from the start. And achieving success will enlarge the community's pool of memories, thus enriching the shared sense of identity that binds a community together in the first place.

CHAPTER 4

Community Oral History Tools and Technology

In its contemporary form, oral history has evolved alongside the recording technology that makes it possible to capture voices—and images—and save them for tomorrow. Additionally, the evolution of computer technology and the creation of the Internet have added new tools that make oral historians' tasks easier. But in all cases, it's important to remember that technological tools are just that: tools to help you accomplish your goals. They never should be the driving forces behind your decisions on how to plan and carry out a community oral history project.

Technology Decisions

The most cursory visit to an electronics store, a mobile phone vendor, or an online site selling electronic goods is enough to overwhelm would-be oral historians with a plethora of options for recording voices and still or moving images. Devices small enough to get lost in a purse or backpack allow you to record and send voices and photos to people around the globe. But you can cross a lot of those digital devices off your oral history wish list by keeping in mind the fundamental purpose of doing oral history in the first place: conducting interviews to gather and preserve information that will be made accessible to others, not just today but for years to come.

 Don't let technology drive project decisions.

Volume 2 of this *Toolkit, Planning a Community Oral History Project,* will guide you through the technical details of understanding the relative merits of various recording technologies. Given the overarching purpose of doing oral history, the two most important things to remember are:

- Use devices that record audio in uncompressed, non-proprietary formats and record video in low-compression formats whenever possible. This means you will be recording the best quality sound and images, and the recordings will be compatible with many preservation and play-back options.

- Use an external microphone that plugs into the recorder and records equally well the voices of both the interviewer and interviewee. This allows the most flexibility in recorder placement and will maximize the audio quality. You will be able to hear both the questions being asked and the answers—the give and take that is a key characteristic of oral history interviews.

Oral historians also face decisions about whether to record their interviews in audio only or in audio and video. In a 21st century culture described as increasingly visual, the temptation is great to video-record everything. Indeed, many community oral history projects have an important visual component to the extent that they are tied to documenting particular geographic locations, specific elements of the built environment, or unique artistic, cultural or other processes, from glass blowing to lobster fishing. In those cases, video recording is an important part of documenting the context of the oral history interviews. But in other situations where community oral history projects are without a particular visual tie, video recordings of oral history interviews likely will result in a series of visually uninteresting talking heads.

Certainly there may be merit in recording the visual images of oral history interviewees along with their voices. Sometimes, for example, interviewees have particularly engaging speaking styles that make their talking heads anything but boring. Video recordings might expand the options for creating secondary uses of the interviews, such as using them in documentaries, on websites, or in museum exhibits. And family members of oral history interviewees might treasure a video recording of an older relative after she dies. All of that, of course, also could be true of audio recordings.

Oral history planners, however, need to take into account the realities of video recording at a level of quality that will stand up over time. Video equipment that will record in a high-quality format can be more expensive than audio recorders, and because digital video creates very large files, it also can present challenges for preservation and access. And occasionally, community oral history historians find that prospective interviewees are unenthusiastic about being video recorded, perhaps because they are self-conscious about their appearance or for some other reason.

Maintenance requirements and ease of use are other factors that play into oral history equipment decisions. Although a low-budget community project may not be able to afford top-of-the-line equipment, it may be able to borrow good quality recorders that are owned and maintained by the local school district, a community college, a museum, or the local historical society. A community oral history project that will rely on some technology-challenged or perhaps visually-impaired volunteers, as interviewers may decide that ease of use is one of the most important equipment considerations. But a project able to count on the services of an experienced videographer likely would make very different equipment choices.

All of these issues need to be taken into consideration when determining what kind of recording technology to use. **Volume 2,** *Planning a Community Oral History Project,* will help you weigh the various factors to find the proper balance for your particular community oral history project and its specific needs, all the while keeping in mind the admonition that the tools themselves should serve the project's ends, never drive the project. And whatever recording technology a project chooses, make sure all your interviewers are thoroughly trained and completely comfortable with it. They need to know how to operate the equipment and how to trouble-shoot problems that might arise. Projects that choose to video record interviews sometimes find it useful to have two people involved in each interview: one person to operate the video equipment and one person to ask the questions and, often, to operate a separate audio recorder. **Volumes 3** and **4** of the *Toolkit* discuss interviewer training in detail, emphasizing the importance of interviewers having plenty of time to practice using whatever recording devices the project has chosen.

Sometimes other technology issues arise for oral history projects when a person who would be an appropriate interviewee isn't available locally for a face-to-face interview. Occasionally an interviewer from the project can travel to conduct the interview in person. When that's not possible, modern technology may seem to offer solutions, and you may be tempted to consider an interview by long-distance telephone, a video-conferencing-type session, or even an exchange of questions by email.

Here again, it's important to keep in mind the overarching purpose: The intent of your project is to collect oral history information in an interview setting for the purpose of preserving it and making it available to others.

Certainly telephone interviews can be recorded, with the interviewee's permission, but the quality is likely to be diminished and the interviewer will not have the benefit of nonverbal cues by the interviewee that can signal when follow-up questions are critical. Video-conferencing technology may allow for two-way exchanges to be recorded and retrieved, but the quality may not meet long-term preservation and access standards. Finally, an email exchange or real-time chat online isn't an oral history interview at all. Although such online communications can be a useful way to collect information and information submitted by email can be part of a community history collection, this methodology should not be considered oral history. Such an approach lacks the face-to-face spontaneity that occurs when two people sit in the same room and talk with each other using the structured, planned interview outline that is characteristic of oral history interviews. As well, variables such as keyboarding skills and facility with written language likely would result in very different kinds of answers than an interviewer would hear if asking questions orally and in person. Finally, the oral historian cannot truly be sure who is on the other end of an email exchange.

Record-keeping Decisions

In addition to recording equipment, community oral history projects need other technology tools to plan and manage their work as it unfolds. *Planning a Community Oral History Project* (**Volume 2 of the** *Toolkit)* **and** *Managing a Community Oral History Project* (**Volume 3**) provide detailed information and guidance on these other tools. In brief, project technology considerations need to include the kind of record-keeping system you'll need to keep track of the many moving parts an oral history project has when it's in full swing.

Most community oral history projects find it essential to have a computer with basic word-processing capability and people who know how to use it. Projects need to be able to write letters to potential donors, potential volunteers, potential interviewees, and others involved with the project. They also need to be able to create necessary paperwork, such as legal release agreements, that is critical to the project's operation. Even a project that expects to interview only a handful of people will find it useful to create computer files to keep track of who has been contacted for an interview, which volunteers have attended training, who has been assigned as the interviewer, when the interview took place, when the transcript was reviewed, and so forth. The many steps in planning and managing a community oral history project require planners to anticipate record-keeping needs ahead of time and prepare to handle them efficiently. The appendices in this volume and the information in **Volumes 2, 3, and 5** of the *Toolkit* provide detailed information to help oral history projects through this process.

Assessing the technology and record keeping needs of a community oral history project can seem daunting at the outset, particularly when the rapidly changing world of digital recording devices renders your brand new recorder obsolete almost as soon as you take it out of its box. But as long as your project remains focused on its goals, you'll be able to make choices that will lead to high-quality recordings that will stand the test of time.

CHAPTER 5

Preserving and Using Oral History Materials

When you sort through Grandma's attic or basement, too often you'll find a cache of shoeboxes stuffed with letters written by people whose names you don't recognize and snapshots of unidentified people you've never laid eyes on. And Grandma was the last person who could have told you who those people were. Don't let that happen to the materials your community oral history project will generate.

People involved in a community oral history project often begin with infectious enthusiasm for getting out and starting to conduct interviews. That's great, but only if you can first harness that enthusiasm enough to think through and plan the entire project before turning on the recorders. And a critical part of the planning is addressing what you will do with the interviews after the recorder is turned off.

Community oral history projects frequently are motivated by a desire to achieve a specific outcome or create a specific public product: a video to play at an anniversary celebration, a museum exhibit, a centennial book, or a play or other stage performance. Those are important outcomes for oral history projects. But it's important to remember that they represent secondary uses of the primary oral history document—the full interview—and, at best, they only include a portion of the information that was collected.

Community oral historians need to remember the two-fold purpose of doing oral history: to preserve the information for the future as well as to make it accessible to others. The publications, public presentations, or performances derived from oral history interviews are excellent examples of immediate accessibility, but an equal concern for the long-term preservation will assure ongoing accessibility for generations to come. And addressing long-term preservation issues is best accomplished at the beginning of a project. Don't wait until you have the interviews in hand before deciding

Interviews Can Yield Many Veins of Information to Mine

One oral history project of the Cushman Motor Works in Lincoln, Nebraska, aimed to document workers' experiences at the plant for its 100th anniversary celebration. The project included interviews with the first African-American employee to move to a non-foundry job and with women who entered the workforce at the plant in large numbers during World War II. The project published a centennial history book and created a photo exhibit in connection with the anniversary celebrations, but the interviews themselves included more than the published information. People interested in what life was like in Lincoln's small African-American community in the mid-20th century, in the roles of women, or in the details of factory safety and emergency medical care, for example, could glean fascinating insights from the full interviews.[13]

what to do with them. Moreover, many public libraries have a mission to be involved in the local community and are happy to partner with community oral history projects to further that mission.

Determining a Repository at the Outset

Community oral history projects derive at least three important advantages when they identify and work with a repository from the outset. First, a library, archives, or museum that is willing to accept oral history materials might have the technical expertise needed to determine the most appropriate recording technology to use to meet optimal preservation standards. Some repositories, in fact, might not accept oral history materials that do not meet particular technical standards, so determining these requirements before decisions are made about which recording devices to use could be critical. Additionally, some libraries or local museums that already maintain oral history collections might have recording equipment available to lend to community oral history projects.

Second, identifying a repository from the outset could help streamline the process of developing an oral history legal release agreement. The need for such documents and how they are used is discussed extensively in **Volumes**

2 and 4 of the *Community Oral History Toolkit*. Museums, archives, and any other kinds of repositories that accept materials from donors generally have standard legal documents by which the owners of such materials sign over the items to the repository and detail any stipulations associated with the donation. A repository that already holds an oral history collection likely will have legal release agreements it requires for oral history donations; even if a repository doesn't already have an oral history collection, it will doubtless be familiar with the need to develop appropriate legal release agreements. That may make the community oral history project's job easier, but it will still be important to determine whether the repository's policies are a good fit with a particular project's goals.

Finally, identifying—and using—an appropriate repository is the best way to assure ongoing preservation of and access to materials a community oral history project generates. The people originally involved with a community oral history project won't be around forever, and an appropriate repository is much more likely than a small community group to be in a position to keep up with the technological changes needed to assure ongoing access to the oral histories. You may be tempted to think that just putting the oral histories on a website is the solution. However, while Web publication offers access, it is not the equivalent of repositories, including digital archives, which will aim for long-term preservation of the interviews and all the materials associated with them. Again, **Volume 5** provides an extensive discussion of these points.

Processing Oral History Materials

Regardless of the decisions community oral history project teams make about identifying a repository, considerable work with the recordings and other interview materials is needed before the collection can be turned over to a repository. The remaining volumes of the *Toolkit* discuss aspects of this work assigned to various project participants. For example, legal release agreements need to be signed after each interview session; recordings need to be copied and appropriately labeled and the originals set aside for safekeeping; summaries of the interview content need to be written; and the circumstances of the interviews and technical details of the recording need to be documented.

 Verbatim transcripts turn spoken language into written language.

The *Community Oral History Toolkit* advocates that oral history interviews all be transcribed verbatim. Creating a verbatim transcript of an oral history interview is the process of turning spoken language into written language, complete with the conventions of written language, such as punctuation, sentences, and paragraphs, which generally are not characteristics of spoken language. The process is laborious and time consuming, generally taking from six to eight hours to transcribe a one-hour interview. Speakers with accents or hard-to-understand speaking styles or recordings with less-than-optimal sound clarity can present particular challenges in creating verbatim transcripts. Moreover, transcribers may find it impossible to convey the nonverbal communication that occurs when speakers pause, cry, laugh, shout, or otherwise express meaning with tone of voice.

In early days of the evolution of oral history, when recordings were made on reel-to-reel magnetic tape, oral history projects routinely created transcripts and then recorded over the interviews, reusing the tapes. That long ago ceased to be a usual practice, of course, and many projects preserve both the recording as well as verbatim transcripts. Some people in the oral history community now advocate relying primarily on the audio version of the interview rather than a transcript, suggesting that the relative ease of publishing audio and video documents online makes it possible for anyone to listen to an entire original recording, preserving the aural information in addition to the words themselves. Sophisticated computer software also makes it possible to index audio files in such a way that allows topical or keyword searches of oral history interviews.

Online accessibility of audio and video oral history interviews certainly creates opportunities for deeper, more nuanced understanding of interview content, because the recordings expose the nonverbal aspects of communication that occur in the interview setting. But this advantage does not mean oral history projects should abandon verbatim transcription of interviews. Creating transcripts, if at all possible, makes it much easier for researchers, now and in the future, to use oral history material, because most people can read a transcript much faster than they can listen to an interview recording. Ideally, while reading the transcript, they could identify portions of an interview that they could then listen to on the recording, if they chose to do so. Further, a verbatim transcript allows project managers to send a copy to the interviewee for review and ask for corrections of proper names, for example. Sometimes during this review process interviewees will think of additional information that can be added in a footnote to the transcript. Most importantly, however, a written transcript printed on acid-free paper will have the longest-known preservation life compared to evolving digital technologies.

Decades, even centuries, from now, the words of interviewees recorded—and transcribed—today will offer a glimpse of the particular time and place documented by your community oral history project.

Creating Secondary Products

In addition to assuring long-term preservation of community oral histories, most projects devote considerable effort to the additional goal of creating secondary works for public access to the interview information. **Volume 5, *After the Interview in Community Oral History*,** details a number of examples of such oral history-based spinoffs, and even the most cursory computer searches will yield many more examples. Ultimately, of course, the options are limited only by your imagination. Consider the merits of using oral history materials to create

- books, booklets, pamphlets, maps, tourist guides
- audio tours of historic neighborhoods
- quilts, banners, and other artworks
- permanent or traveling exhibits at museums, libraries, or other public spaces
- plays, skits, monologues, and other theater performances
- musical compositions, songs, and dances
- curricula, study guides, and multimedia presentations for schools.

What's more, community oral history projects can have a way of generating more community oral history projects. Finally, the experience you gain from successfully planning and carrying out a project may inspire others to turn to you for advice as they seek to use oral history to document another important aspect of a community's life and times.

CHAPTER 6

Ethical Considerations for Oral Historians

People who embark on a community oral history project are engaging in an endeavor that can have a profound impact on the lives of those who participate in it. As a result, community oral historians need to remain mindful of ethical considerations at every stage of the process.[14] The oral history interview, of course, is the centerpiece of oral history projects. And while many community oral historians probably get started on projects without knowing exactly what an oral history interview sounds like, most probably surmise, intuitively, that oral historians don't act like reporters for supermarket tabloid newspapers, undercover investigators, or hard-boiled county prosecutors.

What community oral historians may not stop to think about, however, is that oral history projects raise ethical issues from the time the project idea is hatched and that navigating those issues needs to be part of the decision-making framework from initial development to final archiving and public programming. The ethical underpinnings of oral history are based on respect for interviewees who consent to share a slice of their lives with an oral historian. **Volume 4,** *Interviewing in Community Oral History*, explores in detail the ethics of the oral history interview. But community oral historians also should keep in mind ethical considerations in their decisions on:

- framing an oral history project,
- selecting audio or video recording equipment,
- choosing a repository for their oral history materials,
- securing legal release agreements from each interviewee,
- obtaining project funding, and
- documenting the historical context of the interviews.

The ethical underpinnings of oral history are based on respect for interviewees.

This chapter introduces these considerations, providing references to subsequent volumes with more expansive information.

Framing an Oral History Project

Volume 2, *Planning a Community Oral History Project* discusses in detail the practical importance of writing a mission statement that clearly articulates the scope of the community oral history project. A mission statement answers the question of what exactly you're trying to do and why. If you cannot adequately spell out the focus of the project, not only will it become unmanageable but it also may be of little use to the historian of 2075 who stumbles across your project in a yet-to-be-invented high-tech archival medium or perhaps even on somewhat musty but entirely readable acid-free paper. Here's why: The historians of 2075—including the great-grandchild doing family history research or the school children studying their community—will be unable to understand the context of the interviews unless you set the stage adequately at the outset. Without the context of the interviews, the content becomes less meaningful. And that's true whether the researcher is looking at your materials in 2075 or next year.

So the first ethical challenge for community oral historians is to be up front with themselves and their audiences—contemporary or yet unborn—about what it is they're trying to accomplish and, perhaps, what they're *not* trying to do. Consider the following example of a clearly stated project focus and purpose that provide sufficient context for any future user to understand what the project planners set out to do and why. The website of the Buffalo Trace Oral History Project at the Louie B. Nunn Center for Oral History at the University of Kentucky Libraries states that the project "is designed to preserve the story of the Buffalo Trace Distillery in Frankfort, Kentucky."[15] The website also states that, in the project interviews, "we are given an insider's look at life in the distillery and how world-class bourbon is made," making very clear what this project is all about, and what it's *not* about. Anyone reading this introductory statement can be reasonably sure that the interviews do not explore the efforts of groups attempting to restrict alcohol sales to minors or fight drunken driving, both of which would be fertile ground for community oral history projects. That's clearly not part of the Buffalo Trace project's interviews.

Consider Built-in Biases

One New York City-based project aimed to collect information from longtime squatters to enable homeless people to engage in grassroots action to acquire vacant housing. A post on the H-Oralhist listserv said an interview with a celebrated squatter was "done with the intent to contribute to that process" of promoting squatting—a clear statement of purpose.[16] But perhaps it would be more accurate to describe this not as oral history but as using interviews to further social activism. This is not the same as an oral history project that would attempt to include interviews with city officials who enforce housing codes, policymakers who created the codes in the first place, property owners or managers whose buildings are squatted in, and other players in this complex urban drama—all of which would create a comprehensive picture of this issue.

In recent years, community groups and advocacy organizations have turned to oral history methodology to provide virtually immediate, real-time documentation of ongoing situations or events, much like journalists, with projects that focus on 9/11, Hurricane Katrina, devastating tornadoes, and other natural and man-made disasters around the world. The need to articulate the scope and purpose becomes even more critical for understanding the context of oral history projects when they have overt or inadvertent political purposes. Such projects make ethical decisions, if they openly acknowledge their particular biases and if they recognize there may be other legitimate, if contradictory, viewpoints.

Often projects designed to promote social activism goals or based on other real-time documentation efforts tend to evoke strong emotions, particularly because the subjects of the inquiry are an ongoing reality for the interviewees. But recording emotions alone is not oral history. Rather, the oral historian is ethically obligated to go beyond the emotions and explore the interviewee's understanding of the subject at hand.

Such projects also raise significant ethical concerns related to the potential for exploiting vulnerable people. The well-known slave narratives collected in the 1930s, a precursor of modern oral history, illustrate the dangers here. Scholars who have analyzed the accounts of interviews with some of the former slaves have concluded that, at least in some cases, the interviewees had no clear understanding of the purpose of the interviews and apparently believed the white interviewers represented social services agencies that could help ameliorate their poverty-stricken lives.[17]

Selecting Audio or Video Recording Equipment

Determining what recording devices to use is one of the early decisions community oral history project planners have to make. **Volume 2,** *Planning a Community Oral History Project*, provides a wealth of technical information to guide that decision. Part of the decision-making process includes consideration of the ethical component attached to the selection and use of oral history recording equipment.

Video cameras that are intrusive and used amateurishly, inexpensive audio recorders that produce garbled, inaudible sound, and camera positions and lighting (either still or video) that result in needlessly unflattering photos all are examples of oral history efforts that ignore the basic ethical standard of respect for interviewees.

One significant advantage of contemporary technological advances is that sophisticated but mostly user-friendly recording devices are increasingly available at reasonable prices, if only the oral historian will take the time to learn how to use them appropriately. Failure to do so can result in numerous technical problems, all of which can threaten the long-term preservation of the recordings. Here again is the ethical issue: Interviewees are being asked to give of themselves, but if their gift evaporates because of inadequate or misused recording devices, the oral historian has broken the fundamental trust between interviewer and interviewee.

Choosing a Repository for Oral History Materials

Fundamental ethical concerns also lie at the heart of another early decision community oral historians make, namely who will own the materials their oral history project generates, a matter discussed fully in **Volumes 2 and 5** of the *Community Oral History Toolkit*. Interviewees who participate in an oral history project are giving part of themselves when providing an account of their experiences and their understandings of those experiences. Ethical oral historians understand their obligation to preserve those accounts in their entirety, so they may be available to others both today and for generations to come.

Maintaining an oral history collection is a significant undertaking in light of today's rapid, ongoing technological change. Will the repository receiving the oral history materials be in a position to assure ongoing access in light of evolving technological changes that inevitably will make some forms of recording and preservation obsolete? In other words, how can the project assure its materials will be available over the long term, which is essential for a community oral history project to do justice to the men and women who freely share part of themselves in oral history interviews?

Securing Legal Release Agreements From Every Interviewee

Oral history interviews are documents deemed to be copyrightable under federal law. Both the interviewee and interviewer whose voices are on the recording, hold a copyright interest in the recording. So oral history projects that intend to use these materials in some sort of public presentation or put them in a repository where others may use them, generally ask both interviewee and interviewer to assign their copyright interests to the project sponsors or repository by means of a legal release agreement. All the remaining volumes of the *Community Oral History Toolkit* elaborate on various aspects of this legal requirement.

In addition to the legal ramifications of such documents, important ethical questions are associated with the content of those release agreements. Has the interviewee been fully informed about what the project sponsors plan to *do* with the materials, particularly in regard to creating public programming or publishing the materials on the Web? Does the document respect interviewees' interests, including allowing them to refuse to authorize such publication or restrict the interview's use in any other way?

Although these questions have ramifications for drafting legal release agreements, they are fundamentally ethical issues that speak to the general principle of respecting people who agree to be interviewed. That respect extends to recognizing that interviewees may not all share the project team's enthusiasm for online publication of oral history materials. The reverse, of course, might also be true: with the prospect of everyone on the globe having access to an interview, some interviewees' visions of fame—or perhaps notoriety—might modify the content of their interview in such a way as to raise doubts about its veracity. If project sponsors suspect that's the case, do they have an ethical obligation to indicate that in their published materials?

Obtaining Project Funding

Community oral historians sometimes have to walk an ethical tightrope as they work to secure funding for oral history projects. Oral historians may compete for limited resources, but they also must strive to assure that those who contribute to a project's support—either in cash or in kind—do not exert undue influence on who is interviewed or what subjects the interviews explore. At the same time, it is important that projects give clear public credit to those who underwrite community oral history work. Creating budgets and finding financial support are discussed in detail in **Volumes 2 and 3** of this *Toolkit*.

Documenting Historical Context

Community oral history planners who articulate a clear mission statement at the outset are well on their way to assuring that their project will add important, new information to the historical record. And as a project unfolds, it will continue to uphold ethical standards as long as interviewers ask thoughtful follow-up questions, explore all aspects of the subject at hand, and thoroughly document the time, place, and circumstances of the oral history interviews.

By establishing the broader historical context of oral history interviews, today's oral historians fulfill an ethical duty to tomorrow's users of the community history being documented now.

Moreover, providing that broader historical context will help people who encounter the oral histories in the future to exercise *their* ethical responsibilities in analyzing and seeking to understand the interviews. The issue of context may become particularly critical to the extent that future users of oral histories rely on online search tools that make it possible to find quite narrow slices of an interview. Reading an entire transcript or listening to an entire tape—the old fashioned way of engaging with an oral history interview—is clearly time consuming, particularly when a researcher is interested in only a specific aspect of an interviewee's account. But it has the distinct advantage of giving the researcher the complete context of the interview. The ability that computer technology affords to drill down into an interview and find narrow, specific segments creates an ethical obligation on the part of people who use oral history interviews to be aware of the very real possibility that such information may readily be taken out of context, thus disserving the intent of the interviewees.

As problematic as some of these issues may appear, thoughtful oral historians can navigate these ethical waters successfully. One example of a community oral history project that has done so is the Rocky Flats Cold War Museum oral history project, whose interviews are housed at the Maria Rogers Oral History Program of the Boulder, Colorado, Carnegie Branch Library for Local History.[18] This project is exemplary on several levels, including the volume of work and complexity of content in addition to the clear ethical underpinnings with which planners approached their work. The focus of the project is a Cold War nuclear weapons plant, which is a subject that evokes strong emotions to this day. And complex, confusing, and sometimes contradictory information is emerging in the interviews. But the oral history project was not designed to reconcile these differences and craft an overarching master narrative about Rocky Flats. Rather, it was to collect information from a comprehensive array of individuals. In short, to allow them to tell their stories.

CHAPTER 7

Exploring Best Practices
for Community Oral History Projects

The *Toolkit's* Best Practices for Community Oral History Projects, which are presented in abbreviated form in the Introduction, appear in all five volumes as a way to remind community oral historians of the fundamental standards that guide the creation of first-rate oral history projects. They distill the key themes introduced in this volume, all of which are elaborated in Volumes 2 through 5. Although some of the underlying ideas have been touched on earlier in this volume, this chapter provides a detailed discussion of the Best Practices and explains why they are important and how they fit into the oral history process.

> 1. **Familiarize yourself with the Oral History Association's guidelines.** First developed in 1968 and revised and updated regularly since then, these guidelines are the benchmark for the practice of ethical oral history and form the foundation on which solid oral history projects are built. Becoming familiar with them will help your project get off to a strong start.

As you will see throughout the *Toolkit,* oral history methods have evolved over the past half-century or so, as scholars from many different disciplines have approached oral history and used its research methods to shed light on the human perspectives that can easily get lost in some other approaches to research. Historians in particular, within and without the halls of academia, have expanded their efforts to understand and document the lives of everyday people in all sorts of communities by turning to the sources who know that history the best: community members themselves. And they create a solid historical record when they conduct their work in accord with the guidelines established by oral history practitioners from around the nation who share their expertise through the national Oral History Association. In fact, agencies that fund oral history projects may look at a proposal to see if planners intend to follow OHA guidelines as one measure of the care and professionalism with which the project has been planned. So familiarizing yourself with the OHA guidelines is a good place to start thinking like a historian.

2. **Focus on oral history as a process.** Using standard historical research methods, you are setting out to explore a historical question through recorded interviews, giving them context and preserving them in the public record—in addition to whatever short-term goals your project may have, such as using interview excerpts to create an exhibit or celebrate an anniversary.

Community oral history projects frequently start with the idea that it would be great to talk to some of the old-timers and create an exhibit of some sort to celebrate a landmark anniversary. Circumstances can vary widely, of course. It might be 50 years since the congregation was founded. It might be 25 years since the local disability rights movement championed greater accessibility in public buildings. Or maybe it's not a celebration, but an attempt to document a neighborhood's history before it gives way to wrecking balls and bulldozers that will leave a shopping mall in their wake. Whatever the immediate spark for the project, it's best to think of an oral history project *not* as merely a series of interviews for a one-time exhibit but as a *process* that allows you to explore a historical question by building on the existing public record and making new information available for others into the future.

3. **Cast a wide net to include community.** Make sure all appropriate community members are involved in your project and have an opportunity to make a contribution. Community members know and care the most about the project at hand, and the more closely they are involved in every aspect of it, the more successful it will be.

Some communities, whether they share physical, emotional, or intellectual space, are tightly knit. Others may have little in common save a shared concern about a particular issue. In both cases, oral history projects contribute more to the historical record if they include the perspectives of as many disparate voices as possible. Even members of tightly knit communities seldom are unanimous in their assessments of past times and events. And often, it is in those disagreements that new understandings emerge, shedding light on shared experiences. Moreover, including a variety of community members who bring different skills along with their enthusiasm for the project will assure buy-in from people with various perspectives on the issue at hand. And that can be crucial as you look for financial and in-kind support at all stages of the oral history project.

4. **Understand the ethical and legal ramifications of oral history.** Oral historians record deeply personal stories that become available in an archive for access both in the present and the future. So oral historians have ethical and legal responsibilities to abide by copyright laws and respect interviewees' wishes while also being true to the purposes of oral history.

Community oral history interviewers aim to document previously unknown information about the community in question, filling in gaps and seeking deeper context about what is already known. And they do so by engaging in intense, one-on-one interview sessions with people who have firsthand knowledge to contribute to the topic at hand. Oral historians ask interviewees, in effect, to give part of themselves, so it's important to keep in mind the ethical practices and legal implications of recording another's words. **Volumes 2 and 4** offer detailed information on ethical and legal issues for community oral historians to consider as they embark on a project.

5. **Make a plan.** At the outset, define your purpose, set goals, evaluate your progress, and establish record-keeping systems so details don't get out of control.

Successful oral history projects always begin with a plan, not an interview. **Volumes 2 and 3** will lead you step by step through the process of planning and managing an oral history project. They'll give you ideas about how to decide what, exactly, you're trying to accomplish and how to organize your human and inanimate resources to reach your goals. As with planning any long-term project, the oral history process will, necessarily, have to have some built-in flexibility. Volunteers may drift away or simply move out of town and no longer be available. Information that emerges from interviews may take the project in a somewhat different direction than initially expected. An overwhelming cache of information may be uncovered that significantly enlarges the potential scope of the work. Oral history projects that begin with a well-thought-out plan and an ability to clearly articulate the project's purpose will be able to deal with unexpected developments much more readily than those whose plans are jotted on the back of an envelope with only the vaguest idea of where they're going—or how they'll know when they've arrived.

> **6. Choose appropriate technology with an eye toward present and future needs.** Technology is necessary for recording interviews, preserving them in an archive, and providing access and using them for public displays. Make wise decisions about the technology you use.

Oral history is a technology-intensive pursuit. In fact, the history of oral history closely aligns with the evolution of audio recording devices, beginning around World War II and expanding rapidly thereafter. In recent years, the explosion of digital technology has made audio and video recording technology readily accessible. Additionally, the ability of virtually anyone to publish digital materials thanks to the World Wide Web has created new layers of opportunity—and new ethical responsibilities—for oral historians. Communities that seek to document themselves using oral history methods are wise to consider both immediate and long-term purposes of collecting oral history as they embark on a project. Those purposes will inform their choice of recording technology and affect their plans for what to do with the oral histories after they've been collected. **Volume 2** of the *Toolkit* explores in detail many aspects of selecting technology appropriate to your project.

7. **Train interviewers and other project participants to assure consistent quality.** Oral history interviews differ from some other interview-based research methods in the amount of background research and preparation required. Make sure interviewers and other personnel are thoroughly trained in oral history principles, interviewing techniques, recording technology and ethics. The *Community Oral History Toolkit* covers all these topics.

Oral history projects that rely on volunteers, as most community projects do, often have eager participants willing to do the many tasks it takes to complete a successful project. But even the most enthusiastic volunteers need training to learn what the project is about—and what it's not about. They need to participate in workshops to learn how to conduct effective oral history interviews, and they need time to practice using equipment the project has chosen. **Volume 4, *Interviewing*,** includes a detailed outline of a sample workshop for training oral history interviewers that will help assure project volunteers embark on their interviews with the background and practice they need to be successful.

8. **Conduct interviews that will stand the test of time.** This is the heart of the oral history process, but its success depends on laying solid groundwork.

Community celebrations, commemorations, or sudden upheavals—either natural or manmade—all can spark community oral history projects. The temptation is often great to dust off whatever recording devices folks have at home, or to run out and buy the newest popular digital gadgets, and get started on some interviews with community members deemed to be in the know. As you'll learn from the five volumes of the *Community Oral History Toolkit,* that approach seldom results in a collection whose content is of lasting historical value. Instead, interviews based on appropriate planning, thorough research, and well-trained interviewers are much more likely to yield content that goes beyond the surface of the community's history and provides context for future generations to gain a deeper understanding of the past.

9. **Process and archive all interview materials to preserve them for future use.** Oral history interviews and related materials should be preserved, cataloged and made available for others to use in a suitable repository, such as a library, archive or historical society.

Our understanding of past times and places relies in large part on the documentary evidence that literate people left behind: medieval church manuscripts, the journals of Lewis and Clark, two centuries of congressional proceedings, pioneer women's diaries from the overland trails. Community oral history projects contribute much the same kind of documentation about past times and places that future historians—and the casually curious—may turn to in an effort to understand more fully the life of your community. That's why it's important to go beyond any immediate goal of creating a public presentation based on your oral history collection. **Volume 5** provides the nuts and bolts of what it takes to assure that your complete oral history collection, not just the excerpts used today, will remain accessible for years to come.

10. **Take pride in your contribution to the historical record.** Share with the community what you've learned, and celebrate your success.

Community oral history projects are always greater than the sum of their parts. Consider the following:

- the handful of enthusiasts who get it started and make a plan;
- the worker bees who make the phone calls, do the research, conduct the interviews, raise the money, and keep track of the files;
- the interviewees who share their knowledge and pieces of their lives;
- the interviewees' families who cherish the recording of Grandpa after he's gone; and
- the teachers who turn to the collection in years to come as they strive to help students explore their community's past.

When the last interview is fully processed and turned over to a repository, everyone associated with your community oral history project should take pride in your collective accomplishments. By keeping your sights on these best practices for community oral history projects and by equipping yourself with the detailed information in this five-volume *Community Oral History Toolkit,* you will have made an important contribution to your community's knowledge and understanding of itself. And generations to come will thank you.

CHAPTER 8

Overview of the
Community Oral History Toolkit

The previous chapters of this volume set the stage for understanding the practice of oral history and what sets it apart from other research methods. The remaining volumes of the *Toolkit* will help you dig into the process in detail. All five volumes complement one another without being overly repetitious. The information in each volume is intended to lead readers to the next volume. This chapter gives you an overview of the detailed information you'll find in the remaining four volumes, presented as checklists that help you see at a glance the kind of tasks that lie ahead.

 Combined, the five *Toolkit* volumes cover everything you need to know to do community oral history.

Volume 2, *Planning a Community Oral History Project*, will lead you through the critical work of laying a solid foundation for a successful project. Many community groups start oral history projects with a great deal of enthusiasm and, in their eagerness, begin by recording interviews with folks they consider wonderful storytellers. That's usually a recipe for failure. Instead, follow the oral history project planning steps described in detail in Volume 2 of the *Toolkit*, and you'll be on your way to a successful project. It will give you the information that you need to work through all of the planning steps and will help you to prepare to manage the project.

COMMUNITY ORAL HISTORY PLANNING STEPS

✓ Form a project planning team and choose a planning director.

✓ Identify community supporters and resource people.

✔ Become familiar with oral history ethical guidelines and legal standards.

✔ Define project goals, focus, scope, and write a mission statement.

✔ Name the project.

✔ Identify suggested team member options and work space needs.

✔ Make repository arrangements.

✔ Develop forms and record-keeping procedures.

✔ Determine equipment options

✔ Develop a project budget and identify possible funding sources.

✔ Recommend after-the-interview options.

✔ Assemble project plan and share it with supporters.

Volume 3, *Managing a Community Oral History Project*, describes in detail the tasks associated with overall project management as well as the specific tasks associated with managing your equipment, your budget and funding sources, your interviews, and the post-interview process. As well, Volume 3 walks you through end-of-project management tasks, including writing a final report and closing out your project books. Finally, it also encourages you to plan an event to thank everyone who was involved and celebrate your success.

COMMUNITY ORAL HISTORY MANAGEMENT STEPS

✔ Choose a project team and director.

✔ Use the Project Design Statement to affirm organization and design.

✔ Use project name, mission statement, focus, and scope as management guides.

✔ Be sensitive to oral history ethical guidelines.

✔ Apply oral history legal standards.

✔ Organize repository/long-term host option arrangements.

✔ Be sensitive to oral history ethical considerations.

✔ Apply oral history legal standards.

✔ Choose project team and director.

✔ Finalize and use forms and record-keeping procedures.

✓ Finalize and make provisions for project space needs.

✓ Maintain contact with community supporters and draw on expertise of community resource people.

✓ Decide on recording equipment.

✓ Finalize project budget guidelines and utilize available funding sources.

✓ Finalize orientation and workshop materials and lead training sessions.

✓ Manage interview steps.

✓ Process interviews.

✓ Assemble interviews and support materials for preservation and access.

Volume 4, ***Interviewing in Community Oral History***, details the assignments project teams and interviewers need to accomplish before turning on a recorder to conduct an oral history interview. It also fully describes how to conduct an interview and what to do after the recorder is turned off. Volume 4 will give you the detailed information that you need to prepare for and conduct meaningful oral history interviews and will lead you into the post-interview processing steps described in detail in the final volume. The first checklist for Volume 4 sets out what oral history project teams need to do before sending people out to conduct interviews; the second checklist covers what interviewers need to do before turning on their recorders, while recording and afterwards.

WHAT PROJECT TEAMS NEED TO DO

Before the interview

✓ Develop background research materials for interviewers.

✓ Create a timeline, as appropriate, for the project's focus.

✓ Identify potential interviewees and contact them about the project.

✓ Recruit and train interviewers.

✓ Match interviewers with interviewees.

WHAT INTERVIEWERS NEED TO DO

Before the interview

✓ Become familiar with the project and its goals.

✓ Get training so you can use the equipment, learn interviewing techniques.

✓ Do general background research about the project's topic and specific research about your interviewee.

✓ Prepare an outline of topics to pursue in the interview.

✓ Use appropriate recordkeeping forms developed for your project to document information about your interviewee and the interview process and to secure the interviewee's consent.

✓ Schedule the interview.

✓ Arrive on time and bring everything you need.

✓ Arrange the interview setting to achieve the best possible audio or video quality.

During the interview

✓ Make sure the interviewee is comfortable.

✓ Check your equipment to be sure it's working properly.

✓ Record a standard introduction.

✓ Use the topic outline to guide questions.

✓ Ask follow-up questions for details and context.

✓ Use appropriate oral history interviewing techniques.

After the interview

✓ Sign the interview legal release agreement.

✓ Photograph the interviewee.

✓ Thank the interviewee.

✓ Write a summary of the interview.

✓ Complete all remaining interview-related tasks as determined by project teams.

Volume 5, *After the Interview in Community Oral History*, will provide the information you need to preserve your interviews as a coherent, permanent collection that will be accessible to those who want to know more about the community whose history you have documented. This volume will equip you with the tools that you need to effect the transition from interviews to permanent collection. Although Volume 5 introduces concepts and vocabulary that may be unfamiliar to people who are not librarians or archivists, it provides clear definitions. Volume 5 also includes examples of a variety of community oral history projects and outlines how they have shared the results of their efforts through public presentations based on information gleaned from the interviews. These examples will give you insights about how oral history projects can enrich communities through shared experiences.

COMMON INTERVIEW PROCESSING STEPS

✓ Begin a "log" for each interview as soon as it is completed.
✓ Copy the recording and label all copies of recording media. Store the copies safely.
✓ Transcribe each interview according to project guidelines.
✓ Prepare the oral history for the repository.
✓ Prepare the oral history for website.
✓ Send official thank-you notes to the interviewees on behalf of the project.
✓ Record the successful completion of the oral histories and file all master documents.

Taken together these five volumes provide a comprehensive guide to planning and carrying out a community oral history project. I hope you'll use them to launch your project. It will require hard work, of course—most important tasks do—but it also can be great fun. You'll be equipped with solid information on how to proceed and what it takes to create oral histories that remain accessible over time and make a difference in the life of your community. You'll be creating a gift for the future by helping to preserve a part of your community's past.

Work hard. Have fun. Good luck!

Sample Forms for Managing Oral History Projects

This section of the *Community Oral History Toolkit* contains sample forms to help you plan and manage an oral history project, both before and after the interviews. You can also find them online and download them directly from **www.LCoastPress.com** (go to the *Community Oral History Toolkit* page). Using them will help you defuse frustration and stay on top of the myriad details an oral history project inevitably entails. Maintaining appropriate records as a project evolves is critical. And when it comes time to wind down and turn materials over to a library or other repository, you'll be glad you did.

The sample forms are all straightforward and easy to use. You may not need all of them, and you likely will want to adapt some of them to your particular situation. Pay special attention to the legal release agreements: they are offered solely as samples and should not be construed as offering legal advice to your project.

In addition to the unpopulated forms in this appendix, you'll find examples of the same forms, but filled in, scattered throughout the *Toolkit* volumes illustrating how they should be used.

Sample Form Templates

Templates for all of these forms can be found online at **www.LCoastPress. com** (go to the *Community Oral History Toolkit* page). These templates can guide the planning and implementing of an oral history project. Adapt them to your own needs.

Sample Project Forms

Project Design Statement
(*See p. 77 for sample; download a template at* **www.LCoastPress.com**)
This form helps organize ideas for an oral history project and create a road-map for moving forward. Begin your project with this form and use it as a planning tool. *See Volumes 2, 3, and 5.*

Interviewee Recommendation Form
(*See p. 78 for sample; download a template at* **www.LCoastPress.com**)
This form is handy for selecting interviewees. Using a single form such as this can assemble all the information about a potential interviewee in a for-mat that can be "pitched" to a selection committee. *See Volumes 2 and 3.*

Interviewee Biographical Profile
(*See p. 79 for sample; download a template at* **www.LCoastPress.com**)
This form organizes all the relevant biographical information about each in-terviewee and ensures that the same information is collected about each per-son and is available in one place. Different kinds of biographical data are rel-evant for different projects, so adapt it to your needs. *See Volumes 2, 3, 4, and 5.*

Interview Summary
(*See p. 80 for sample; download a template at* **www.LCoastPress.com**)
This form records information about the interview event, specifically, about the recording process, physical environment where the interview takes place, and the content of the interview. It is best filled out by the interviewer im-mediately after the interview. *See Volumes 2, 3, 4, and 5.*

Photograph and Memorabilia Receipt
(*See p. 81 for sample; download a template at* **www.LCoastPress.com**)
Sometimes during the course of an interview, the interviewee will offer ma-terial items such as photographs or scrapbooks to accompany the interview. Sometimes these are offered as gifts but most often they are loans for the project to copy and return. This form can serve as a receipt while the loaned item is in the hands of the interviewer or project. *See Volumes 2, 3, and 4.*

Interview Tracking Form
(*See p. 82 for sample; download a template at* **www.LCoastPress.com**)
This form lists all the tasks required for processing a recorded interview into a

finished oral history. The steps required for every project are different, so adapt the form to your own needs. Many projects prefer to track processing on a spreadsheet, which is easy to set up to mirror this form. *See Volumes 2, 3 and 5.*

Transcription Protocol
(*See p. 83 for sample; download a template at* **www.LCoastPress.com**)
This form defines the specifications for transcribing interviews, including the resources needed and the specific responsibilities of the transcriber. A single transcription protocol is used for the entire project. *See Volume 5.*

Cataloging Protocol
(*See p. 84 for sample; download a template at* **www.LCoastPress.com**)
This form should be filled out jointly by representatives from the oral history project and the repository. Using this written document for the entire project will minimize misunderstanding and keep cataloging consistent for the duration of the project. *See Volume 5.*

Cataloging Work Sheet
(*See p. 85 for sample; download a template at* **www.LCoastPress.com**)
This form needs to be completed for every oral history, and will accompany the interview recording and transcript through cataloging. Detail and accuracy in this form are very important as the information on it will be transferred to the catalog record and subsequent publications. *See Volume 5.*

Sample Agreement Forms

This series of forms consists of sample agreements commonly used in oral history projects. The forms will guide you developing your own agreements, but remember, they are samples only. Each letter of agreement should be adapted to the specific project.

Legal Release Agreement
(*See p. 86 for sample; download a template at* **www.LCoastPress.com**)
This is the most important form in an oral history project. Without a Legal Release Agreement signed by the interviewee and the interviewer, an oral history interview may not legally be used in any way. Every Legal Release agreement should be customized for the particular circumstances of the project. We offer this as a sample. Have a separate agreement signed for *every interview. See Volumes 2, 3, 4, and 5.*

Legal Release Agreement (Restrictions)
(See p. 87 for sample; download a template at **www.LCoastPress.com**)
Occasionally, special cases concerning the interview come up that aren't covered in the generic legal release agreement. Examples are an interviewee's wish that the interview be restricted from public view for a certain amount of time, a request that his name be withheld, and a request that the interview not be made available on the Internet. Though there are many legitimate reasons for placing restrictions on an interview, they should be the exception rather than the rule and the project director should consult with the repository contact as well as a legal advisor before agreeing to one or more restrictions. Adapt this form to specify the restrictions placed on the interview. *See Volumes 3 and 5.*

Letter of Agreement for Repository
(See p. 88 for sample; download a template at **www.LCoastPress.com**)
This agreement spells out the relationship between the oral history project and the repository. It is very important to specify, in writing, which agency is responsible for which tasks, for the expenses incurred, and for maintaining the timeframe. *See Volumes 2 and 3.*

Letter of Agreement for Interviewer
(See p. 89 for sample; download a template at **www.LCoastPress.com**)
A written agreement such as this emphasizes the professional nature of being an interviewer, and also serves are a backup in case there are misunderstandings. *See Volumes 2 and 3.*

Letter of Agreement for Transcriber
(See p. 90 for sample; download a template at **www.LCoastPress.com**)
This letter clarifies the expectations for the transcriber. Usually a single letter for each project transcriber is sufficient. *See Volumes 2, 3, and 5.*

Project Design Statement

This form helps organize ideas for an oral history project and create a road-map for moving forward. Begin your project with this form and use it as a planning tool. *See Volumes 2, 3, and 5.*

PROJECT DESIGN STATEMENT	
GENERAL	
PROJECT NAME	
SPONSORING INSTITUTION	
PRIMARY GOAL	
MISSION STATEMENT	
ADMINISTRATIVE REQUIREMENTS	
PROJECT CONTENT	
HISTORICAL FOCUS	
SCOPE	
TOPICS	
SOURCES FOR BACKGROUND RESEARCH	
PROJECT MANAGEMENT	
DURATION	
NUMBER OF INTERVIEWEES	
RECORDING PLAN	
PHYSICAL SPACE NEEDS	
EXPENSES	
RESOURCES	
INTERVIEWEE RECRUITMENT	
REPOSITORY PLAN	
ONLINE ACCESS FOR INTERVIEWS	
Submitted by	Date
Revised by	Date

Interviewee Recommendation Form

This form is handy for selecting interviewees. Using a single form such as this can assemble all the information about a potential interviewee in a format that can be "pitched" to a selection committee. *See Volumes 2 and 3.*

INTERVIEWEE RECOMMENDATION FORM	
PROJECT NAME	
NAME	**CONTACT**
PLACE OF RESIDENCE	**DATE OF BIRTH**
RELEVANCE TO THE PROJECT (How will this person's life history relate to the goals of the project?)	
BIOGRAPHICAL SUMMARY (family, education, professional experience, and community activities, as relating to the project)	
RECOMMENDED BY	**CONTACT**

ACTION	
_____ *Approved* _____ *Not Approved*	*INITIAL MEETING DATE*
INTERVIEWER	
INTERVIEW DATE AND LOCATION	

Interviewee Biographical Profile

This form organizes all the relevant biographical information about each interviewee and ensures that the same information is collected about each person and is available in one place. Different kinds of biographical data are relevant for different projects, so adapt it to your needs. *See Volumes 2, 3, 4, and 5.*

INTERVIEWEE BIOGRAPHICAL PROFILE	
PROJECT NAME	
NAME	CONTACT
OTHER NAMES KNOWN BY	DATE/PLACE OF BIRTH
PLACE OF RESIDENCE	YEARS IN THE COMMUNITY
OCCUPATION	EDUCATION
RELEVANCE TO THE PROJECT	
RELEVANT BIOGRAPHICAL INFORMATION (AS IT RELATES TO THE GOALS OF THE PROJECT)	
FAMILY (full name, date of birth, relationship to interviewee)	
FRIENDS AND ASSOCIATES (full name, date of birth, relationship to interviewee)	
PLACES TRAVELED OR LIVED	
COMMUNITY ACTIVITIES (Include activity, date, and significance to the project)	
INTERESTS	
INFLUENCES	
LIFE MILESTONES	
Completed by	Date

Interview Summary

This form records information about the interview event, specifically, about the recording process, physical environment where the interview takes place, and the content of the interview. It is best filled out by the interviewer immediately after the interview. *See Volumes 2, 3, 4, and 5.*

INTERVIEW SUMMARY	
PROJECT NAME	INTERVIEW ID#
INTERVIEWEE	INTERVIEWER
NAME (as it will appear in the public record)	NAME
CONTACT	CONTACT
OTHER NAMES KNOWN BY	
INTERVIEW DATE	INTERVIEW LENGTH
RECORDING MEDIUM _____digital audio _____digital video	
DELIVERY MEDIUM _____sound file _____sound card _____ CD _____DVD	
TECHNICAL NOTES (make/model of recorder, format recorded, microphone notes)	
INTERVIEW NOTES (physical environment, interviewee's mood, people or animals in the room, interruptions)	
DATE LEGAL RELEASE AGREEMENT SIGNED _____	
PROPER NAMES AND KEYWORDS (personal and place names with proper spelling, dates, and keywords)	
SUMMARY OF INTERVIEW CONTENT	
COMPLETED BY	DATE

Photograph and Memorabilia Receipt

Sometimes during the course of an interview, the interviewee will offer material items such as photographs or scrapbooks to accompany the interview. Sometimes these are offered as gifts but most often they are loans for the project to copy and return. This form can serve as a receipt while the loaned item is in the hands of the interviewer or project. *See Volumes 2, 3, and 4.*

PHOTOGRAPH AND MEMORABILIA RECEIPT	
PROJECT NAME	
OWNER	
Name	
Address	Phone/Email
ITEM	
Type	Quantity
Detailed Description (Describe item and circumstances of loan)	
Associated Dates	
Physical Condition	
Instructions for use:	
RETURNED	
Items returned by (name):	

OWNER	INTERVIEWER
Name (print)	Name (print)
Signature	Signature
Date	Date

Interview Tracking Form

This form lists all the tasks required for processing a recorded interview into a finished oral history. The steps required for every project are different, so adapt the form to your own needs. Many projects prefer to track processing on a spreadsheet, which is easy to set up to mirror this form. *See Volumes 2, 3 and 5.*

INTERVIEW TRACKING FORM		
PROJECT NAME	**INTERVIEW ID#**	
INTERVIEWEE	**INTERVIEWER**	
NAME	**NAME**	
CONTACT	**CONTACT**	
INTERVIEW DATE		
DATE COMPLETED	**TASK**	**NOTES**
	Log interview recording and assign an interview ID#	
	Log *Legal Release Agreement*	
	Log *Interview Summary*	
	Copy recording	
	Label recording media	
	Transcribe interview	
	Audit-check transcript	
	Check facts and verify spelling of proper names	
	Get interviewee's approval of transcript	
	Complete *Cataloging Work Sheet*	
	Assemble materials for repository	
	Deliver completed oral history to repository	
	Prepare oral history for website	
	Thank Interviewee	
	Archive master files	

Transcription Protocol

This form defines the specifications for transcribing interviews, including the resources needed and the specific responsibilities of the transcriber. A single transcription protocol is used for the entire project. *See Volume 5.*

TRANSCRIPTION PROTOCOL		
PROJECT NAME		
PROJECT CONTACT	Name	Contact
TRANSCRIBER CONTACT	Name	Contact
RESOURCES		
Funds needed		
Equipment needed		
Software needed		
PROCEDURE		
Number of interviews/hours		
Delivery formats		
Delivery method		
Timeframe		
TRANSCRIBER RESPONSIBILITIES	___ Audit-check ___ Summary ___ Verify spelling of proper names ___ Chapter/section headings ___ Index ___ Contents ___ Other (Specify) _____	
STYLE GUIDE		
Project contact – Sign and date		Transcriber contact – Sign and date

Cataloging Protocol

This form should be filled out jointly by representatives from the oral history project and the repository. Using this written document for the entire project will minimize misunderstanding and keep cataloging consistent for the duration of the project. *See Volume 5.*

CATALOGING PROTOCOL		
PROJECT NAME		
PROJECT CONTACT	Name	Contact
CATALOGING CONTACT	Name	Contact
ADMINISTRATIVE		
Organization Sponsoring Oral History Project		
# interviews	**Audio recordings?**	**Transcripts?**
	Video recordings?	**Format:**
Restrictions or special notes on access? Specify		
Note: Signed legal release agreements for each interview must be approved by repository administrator before cataloging begins.		
CATALOG DETAILS		
Destinations for catalog records (include all catalogs, including website)		
Expected completion date		
Encoding format and standards		
Information unit (interview or collection)?		
Controlled vocabulary instructions		
Constant data		
Special Instructions		
Completed by: **Name/Institution**		**Date**
Name/Institution		**Date**

Cataloging Work Sheet

This form needs to be completed for every oral history, and will accompany the interview recording and transcript through cataloging. Detail and accuracy in this form are very important as the information on it will be transferred to the catalog record and subsequent publications. *See Volume 5.*

CATALOGING WORK SHEET		
CONTROLLED FIELDS	✓	Verified
Interviewee's name (100)[1]		
Interviewer's name (700)		
Sponsoring institution (710)		
Subject – Personal names (600)		
Subject – Corporate names (610)		
Subject – Geographic names (651)		
Subject – Topics (650)		
Genre (655)		
UNCONTROLLED FIELDS		
Interview title (245)		
Physical description (300)		
Date and place of interview (518)		
Project name (740)		
Project description (520)		
Interview summary (520)		
Biographical summary (545)		
Keywords (653)		
Prepared by	Date	

[1] The numbers beside the field names refer to the MARC tags which catalogers need to encode the information on this work sheet. Oral historians may ignore them.

Legal Release Agreement

This is the most important form in an oral history project. Without a Legal Release Agreement signed by the interviewee, an oral history interview may not legally be used in any way. Every Legal Release Agreement should be customized for the particular circumstances of the project. We offer this as a sample. Have a separate agreement signed for *every interview. See Volumes 2, 3, 4, and 5.*

LEGAL RELEASE AGREEMENT

The mission of the _____(oral history project) is to document

the history of _____. The major part of this effort is the collection

of oral history interviews with knowledgeable individuals.

Thank you for participating in our project. Please read and sign this gift agreement so your

interview will be available for future use. Before doing so, you should read it carefully and ask any

questions you may have regarding terms and conditions.

AGREEMENT

I, _____ , interviewee, donate and convey my oral history

interview dated _____ to the _____

(oral history project/repository name). In making this gift I understand that I am conveying all right,

title, and interest in copyright to the oral history project/repository. I also grant the oral history

project/repository the right to use my name and likeness in promotional materials for outreach

and educational materials. In return, the oral history project/repository grants me a non-exclusive

license to use my interview through my lifetime.

I further understand that I will have the opportunity to review and approve my interview before it is

placed in the repository and made available to the public. Once I have approved it, the oral

history project/repository will make my interview available for research without restriction. Future

uses may include quotation in printed materials or audio/video excerpts in any media, and

availability on the Internet.

INTERVIEWEE	INTERVIEWER
Name (print) _____	Name (print) _____
Signature _____	Signature _____
Date _____	Date _____

Legal Release Agreement (Restrictions)

Occasionally, special cases concerning the interview come up that aren't covered in the generic legal release agreement. Examples are an interviewee's wish that the interview be restricted from public view for a certain amount of time, a request that his name be withheld, and a request that the interview not be made available on the Internet. Though there are many legitimate reasons for placing restrictions on an interview, they should be the exception rather than the rule and the project director should consult with the repository contact as well as a legal advisor before agreeing to one or more restrictions. Adapt this form to specify the restrictions placed on the interview. *See Volumes 3 and 5.*

LEGAL RELEASE AGREEMENT (RESTRICTIONS)

The mission of the _____(oral history project) is to document

the history of _____. The major part of this effort is the collection

of oral history interviews with knowledgeable individuals.

Thank you for participating in our project. Please read and sign this gift agreement so your

interview will be available for future use. Before doing so, you should read it carefully and ask any

questions you may have regarding terms and conditions.

AGREEMENT

I, _____ , interviewee, donate and convey my oral history

interview dated, _____ to the _____

(oral history project/repository name). In making this gift I understand that I am conveying all right,

title, and interest in copyright to the oral history project/repository. I also grant the oral history

project/repository the right to use my name and likeness in promotional materials for outreach

and educational materials. In return, the oral history project/repository grants me a non-exclusive

license to use my interview throughout my lifetime.

I understand that I will have the opportunity to review and approve my interview before it is placed

in the repository. My gift and the associated rights are subject to the following restrictions:

_____ May not be made available on the Internet

_____ Public access may not be available until (date) _____ _____

_____ Other (specify) _____

INTERVIEWEE	INTERVIEWER
Name (print) _____	Name (print) _____
Signature _____	Signature _____
Date _____	Date _____

Letter of Agreement for Repository

This agreement spells out the relationship between the oral history project and the repository. It is very important to specify, in writing, which agency is responsible for which tasks, for the expenses incurred, and for maintaining the timeframe. *See Volumes 2 and 3.*

LETTER OF AGREEMENT FOR REPOSITORY

This letter summarizes the responsibilities of the _____ (repository) and the _____ (oral history project). In addition to this document, a Legal Release Agreement form signed by each interviewer and interviewee will accompany each oral history.

The _____ **oral history project** is responsible for the following tasks and for the costs incurred:

- Prepare audio- or video-recorded interviews in formats and quality determined by repository
- Transcribe oral history interviews according to style guidelines provided by repository
- Deliver signed Legal Release Agreement for each interview
- Deliver transcript and discs in format agreed upon.

The _____ **repository** is responsible for the following tasks and for the costs incurred:

- Advise in selection and training of interviewers
- Advise in development of project plan
- Catalog oral histories for local catalog and WorldCat
- Format, copy, and bind oral history materials
- Make copies available for use according to repository's access policy.

Number of interviews _____
Timeframe for delivery _____
Number of copies of each interview _____

REPOSITORY	ORAL HISTORY PROJECT
Name (print) _____	Name (print) _____
Signature _____	Signature _____
Title_____	Title_____
Date_____	Date_____

Letter of Agreement for Interviewer

A written agreement such as this emphasizes the professional nature of being an interviewer, and also serves are a backup in case there are misunderstandings. *See Volumes 2 and 3.*

LETTER OF AGREEMENT FOR INTERVIEWER

I, _____, an interviewer for the _____
Oral History Project, understand and agree to the following.

- I understand the goals and purposes of this project and understand I represent the oral history project when I am conducting an interview.

- I will participate in an oral history interviewer training workshop.

- I understand the legal and ethical considerations regarding the interviews and will communicate them to and carry them out with each person I interview.

- I am willing to do the necessary preparation, including background research, for each interview I conduct.

- I will treat each interviewee with respect, and I understand each interview will be conducted in a spirit of openness that will allow each interviewee to answer all questions as fully and freely as he or she wishes.

- I am aware of the need for confidentiality of interview content until such time as the interviews are released for public use per the repository's guidelines, and I will not exploit the interviewee's story.

- I understand my responsibilities regarding any archival materials or artifacts related to the interview that the interviewee may want to include in the interview process.

- I agree to turn all interview materials over to the repository in a timely manner and to help facilitate all necessary processing and cataloging steps.

INTERVIEWER	ORAL HISTORY PROJECT
Name (print) _____	Name (print) _____
Signature _____	Signature _____
Date _____	Date _____

Letter of Agreement for Transcriber

This letter clarifies the expectations for the transcriber. Usually a single letter for each project transcriber is sufficient. *See Volumes 2, 3, and 5.*

LETTER OF AGREEMENT FOR TRANSCRIBER

I, _____ (transcriber), agree to the following:

- Create a verbatim transcript according to style guide provided
- Clearly indicate the interviewee, interviewer, and place and date of the interview at the head of the transcript according to the style guide provided
- Deliver electronic copy in a Microsoft Word 2010 or later document
- Timeframe for delivery _____

The transcription process will include (check all that apply):

_____ Audit-checking the transcript

_____ A reasonable amount of research for correct spelling of proper names

_____ Creating chapter headings

_____ Creating a Table of Contents

_____ Creating an index

_____ Other (Specify) _____

The oral history project will provide a list of proper and place names wherever possible to facilitate accurate transcribing.

As transcriber, I understand that all information contained in the transcript is confidential. I agree not to disclose any information contained in the transcript, nor will I allow anyone access to the recording or the electronic files while they are in my possession. I agree to delete electronic files and destroy discs at the instruction of the oral history project or at the conclusion of the assignment.

TRANSCRIBER	ORAL HISTORY PROJECT
Name (print) _____	Name (print) _____
Signature _____	Signature _____
Title_____	Title_____
Date_____	Date_____

NOTES

1. A significant body of literature about the American West is devoted to compiling and analyzing diaries and letters written by women during the western migration. See, for example, Dee Brown, *The Gentle Tamers: Women of the Old Wild West,* (New York: Putnam, 1958), Julie Roy Jeffrey, *Frontier Women: The Trans-Mississippi West 1840-1880,* (New York: Hill and Wang, 1979), and Joanna L. Stratton, *Pioneer Women: Voices from the Kansas Frontier,* (New York: Simon and Schuster, 1981).

2. Columbia University Oral History Research Office, *Stories from the Collection,* (New York: Columbia University, 1998).

3. For a useful summary of memory research as it relates to oral history, see Valerie Raleigh Yow, *Recording Oral History: A Guide for the Humanities and Social Sciences, 2nd edition,* (Walnut Creek, CA.: AltaMira Press, 2005), pp.35-67.

4. Brian H. Bornstein and Steven D. Penrod, "Hugo Who? G.F. Arnold's Alternative Early Approach to Psychology and Law," published in *Applied Cognitive Psychology,* 22:6 (2008), pp. 759-768.

5. For a discussion of research in this field, see Alistair Thomson, "Memory and Remembering in Oral History," published in *The Oxford Handbook of Oral History,* Donald A. Ritchie, Ed., (New York: Oxford University Press, 2011), pp. 77-95.

6. Yow, *Recording Oral History: A Guide for the Humanities and Social Sciences, 2nd edition,* 51.

7. Laurie Mercier and Madeline Buckendorf, *Using Oral History in Community History Projects,* (Carlisle, PA.: Oral History Association, 2007), 1.

8. See Barbara W. Sommer, *Hard Work and a Good Deal: The Civilian Conservation Corps in Minnesota,* (Minnesota Historical Society Press, 2008).

9. Information about the Arapahoe County, Colorado, oral history project is taken from a presentation at the Oral History Association conference in Atlanta, Oct. 29, 2010, and email correspondence with Cyns Nelson, Feb. 6, 2012.

10. Alexis de Tocqueville, *Democracy in America, Volume II,* Schocken Books Edition (New York: Schocken Books, 1972), pp.128-129.

11. Mary Kay Quinlan, *Hanging On to a Heritage, Forging a Future: The Story of a Farm Community in Transition,* (Unpublished manuscript for Ph.D. dissertation, University of Maryland, 1992).

12. *Ibid.*

13. Mary Kay Quinlan and Barbara W. Sommer, *The People Who Made It Work: A Centennial Oral History of the Cushman Motor Works,* (Lincoln, NE: Textron, Inc., 2001).

14. Portions of this chapter are derived from a conference paper, "Oral History Ethical Dilemmas: More than the Interview" by Mary Kay Quinlan. It was presented at the Oral History Association conference in Atlanta, GA., Oct. 28, 2010.

15. See www.nunncenter.org/buffalotrace/. Accessed June 13, 2012.

16. See "Broadcast OH Interview with Squatter and Activist Frank Morales," July 22, 2009. http://h-net.msu.edu/cgi-bin/logbrowse.pl?trx=vx&list=H-Oralhis t&month=0907&week=d&msg=kFvnz7oWLSG7bnOd%2bCuEhg&user=& pw= Accessed June 13, 2012.

17. See James West Davidson and Mark Hamilton Lytle, *After the Fact: The Art of Historical Detection* (New York: Alfred A. Knopf, 1986).

18. See the special collections at http://www.boulderlibrary.org/oralhistory/ Accessed June 13, 2012.

GLOSSARY

abstract See *summary*.

access The ability of repositories to make information available and to locate it through tools such as finding aids, catalogs, or websites. Access is one of the five principles of good archival practice.

accession The act of formally and legally accepting an item or a collection, such as a collection of oral histories, into a repository.

analog A process that records and stores sound in a continuous pattern. Analog recording is being phased out in favor of digital, both for capture and for preservation, though the majority of oral histories in archives today are analog. Compare to *digital*.

archival quality See *life expectancy*.

archives 1. The actual materials to be saved. 2. The building or repository where archival materials are located. 3. The agency responsible for selecting, acquiring, preserving and making available archival materials.

arrangement The process of organizing materials with respect to their provenance and original order, to protect their context and to achieve physical or intellectual control.

audiocassette An inexpensive and convenient container for audiotape. Audiocassettes were widely used for recording oral histories from the 1960s through the 1990s, and most oral histories in repositories today are stored on audiocassettes.

audit-check Also called audit-edit, transcribers use this term to describe the careful listening and reviewing of the recording done while reading the transcript to catch and correct transcription errors.

binary A numerical system that uses only zeroes (0) and ones (1). All computer applications are based on a binary system.

bit The smallest unit of data used by computers with a single binary value of 0 or 1. A string of eight bits comprises a byte. See also *byte*.

bit rate The number of bits processed in a given unit of time.

Blu-ray An optical disc storage medium designed to supersede DVD format. Blu-ray is capable is a higher definition video image. See also *DVD*.

born digital A document created in a digital format, such as a text document created through word processing, or an interview recorded on a digital recorder.

broadcast quality Recording quality that meets standards for radio or television broadcast.

byte (Technology) A unit of digital information consisting of eight bits. Each byte comprises an alpha-numeric character, and for this reason it is the unit that is most meaningful to humans. See also *bit*.

cardioid microphone See *directional microphone, omnidirectional microphone.*

catalog A "container," usually a database, for catalog records that are related in some way, such as in a library, a digital archive, or a subject database. Records in the catalog can be searched and retrieved.

catalog record The unit within a catalog which describes an item in a collection. In oral history, a catalog record usually defines a single oral history, that is, any number of interviews about a single person.

CD (compact disc) An optical medium for recording and storing data. See also *DVD*.

challenge grant A grant with a defined amount that must be met before funds are distributed.

clip-on microphone See *lavaliere microphone.*

codec Algorithm in a computer program that reduces (compresses) the number of bytes in an electronic file for ease in storing and transmitting data.

collection A group of documents that are related in some way, such as the papers of a person, or an oral history series. The collection should be identified as a unit with a title associated with it.

collection level cataloging Cataloging system that describes an entire collection instead of an individual item, for example, a collection of oral histories. Compare to *item level cataloging*.

collection management system A database software package designed specifically to manage the multiple processes in a repository. See also *management system*.

collection policy A written statement which clearly states the purpose and the boundaries of the repository's collection goals.

community Any group with a shared identity.

community based research Research that takes place in community settings and involves community members in the design and implementation of research projects. Such activities should demonstrate respect for the contributions that are made by community.

compact disc See *CD*.

compressed/uncompressed data See *data compression*.

condenser microphone See *dynamic/condenser microphone*.

consent form See *legal release agreement*.

context The meaning added to something when considered in relation to a larger concept. For example, an oral history of someone within a certain occupational group takes on greater meaning when compared to others of the same occupational group, the same region, or the same time period.

contract A legally binding agreement involving two or more parties, requiring some kind of consideration (payment) and specifying what each party will or will not do. Since oral histories are usually not bought and sold, they are more likely to be exchanged through a deed of gift transaction, which does not require payment. See also *deed of gift*.

controlled vocabulary A tool for improving information retrieval results by using a predetermined list of terms. A thesaurus is one kind of controlled vocabulary. See also *thesaurus*.

copying An important preservation principle referring to copying the content of an oral history. Copies can be made from one format to another, from one medium to another, or to an exact representation of the original. See also *format migration, LOCKSS*.

copyright The exclusive right to reproduce, publish, or sell copies of original creations (such as oral history interviews), and to *license* their production and sale by others. Copyright is granted by the federal government for a limited period of time. When oral histories are accepted into a repository, copyright is often transferred through a *deed of gift*. See also *public domain*, *intellectual property*.

cost-share A division of project costs shared by project and another source or sources.

cross-platform Computer applications that operate on a variety of hardware designs and software programs.

cross-walk A procedure for mapping structured data from one information system to another, for example, from MARC to Dublin Core. The purpose of cross-walks is to share information from one system to another.

cultural heritage The history, beliefs, stories, ceremonies, law, language, symbols, land and artifacts that are shared by a group of people and that make up their culture.

curation The long-term management and care of historical documents and artifacts, in order to ensure maximum access into the indefinite future.

DACS (Describing Archives: a Content Standard) A content standard for describing archives, personal papers, and manuscript collections.

data Information converted into a binary system (zeroes and ones) for digital recording, preservation, and access.

data compression Digital information that is copied to a representation using fewer bits than the original. Data compression results in smaller digital files and sometimes a loss in quality. Oral histories should be recorded and preserved in an uncompressed format, but may be posted on the Internet or played using compressed formats.

data migration The process of transferring data from one format to another.

database A collection of related data that is organized so that its contents can easily be accessed, managed, and updated. Databases are organized by fields, records, and files. A field is a single piece of information; a record is one complete set of fields; and a file is a collection of records.

deed of gift A signed, written agreement which transfers ownership without monetary consideration. Most oral histories are passed from the interviewer or interviewee to the archive through a deed of gift. Compare to *contract*.

defamation A false statement of fact printed or broadcast about a person that tends to injure that person's interest. When the words are printed, the offense is *libel;* when the words are spoken, the offense is *slander*.

description A term used in archival practice for recording information about a resource. The more detailed the description, the easier it is for researchers to find the resource.

digital A process that captures and stores information in discrete values, usually measured in bits (zeroes or ones) and bytes. Compare to *analog*.

digital asset management system System that oversees management and decisions surrounding the acquisition, cataloging, storage, preservation, retrieval and access of a variety of digital files, such as photographs, sound files, video files and text files. See also *management system*.

digital preservation A set of policies, strategies, and actions to ensure access to reformatted and born digital content regardless of the challenges of media failure and technological change. The goal of digital preservation is the accurate rendering of authenticated content over time.

digital repository A permanent, sustainable system of servers with proper management for permanent digital storage. A digital repository often is accessed through a website, but the two are not synonymous.

digital rights management (DRM) An umbrella term to describe the technologies that control and monitor digital content on the Internet. Information may be monitored for reasons of copyright or intellectual property protection, confidentiality, or regulatory compliance. DRM will become an increasingly demanding issue for curators as oral history collections are added to digital archives or on the Internet. See also *management system*.

digital storytelling A popular method for recording and preserving personal or family stories using multimedia.

digitization The act of transferring a sound recording from analog (continuous wave) format to digital (samples of the sound wave converted to bits and bytes).

directional microphone A microphone that picks up sound from a certain direction. The most common type is cardioid, which picks up sound in a heart-shaped field, designed to prevent feedback. Compare to *omnidirectional microphone*.

DVD Originally Digital Video Disc, then Digital Versatile Disc, currently doesn't stand for anything at all. An optical disc used for storing digital information. DVDs hold much more information than CDs but less is known about their preservation qualities. See also *CD, Blu-ray*.

dynamic/condenser microphone A dynamic microphone does not need separate power to operate. It is more durable than a condenser microphone, but less sensitive. A condenser microphone is more sensitive, but requires power, usually from a battery or *phantom power*. See also *microphone*.

EAD (Encoded Archival Description) A metadata standard designed to create digital finding aids for archival materials. See also *metadata.*

external microphone A microphone that is separate from the recording machine. An external microphone is recommended for recording oral history interviews.

fair use A provision in copyright law that allows the limited use of copyrighted materials for teaching, research, scholarship, or news reporting purposes. It is not clear where oral histories fall within this somewhat fuzzy area of the law.

False Memory Syndrome A condition in which a person's identity and relationships are affected by memories that are factually incorrect but are strongly believed. See also *memory*.

file A unit defining related data in a computerized environment, often referred to as a document. Examples of files are text documents, spreadsheets, image files, and audio files.

finding aid The descriptive tool used by archivists to describe a collection of related archival materials. Finding aids generally have a hierarchical design, beginning with a description of a collection, followed by a series within the collection, and ending with item level descriptions within each series.

fiscal sponsor A nonprofit, tax-exempt organization that acts as a sponsor for a project or group that does not have its own tax-exempt status. In the case of a grant, the fiscal sponsor is responsible for reporting back to the foundation on the progress of the project.

folksonomy See *tagging*.

format A fuzzy term used to describe various categories and distinctions in information technology. In the *Toolkit* the term is used as it is in everyday language to a) describe format *categories* such as audio, video, or text formats, as well as b) the distinctions among file formats, such as .wav, .mp3, .pdf. See the Unified Digital Format Registry at http://www.udfr.org/. Format is often confused with medium. See also *medium*.

format migration The process of transferring data from one format to another, usually as part of a digital preservation plan.

foundation A nonprofit, charitable organization.

gift Voluntary transfer of property without getting anything in return. Oral histories are generally transferred to repositories as gifts. See also *deed of gift*.

grant Funds given for a defined purpose. See also *challenge grant*.

hardware Physical components of computers.

high definition (HD) A video system of higher resolution than standard definition (SD). This usually involves display resolutions of involves display resolutions of 1,280×720 pixels (720p) or 1,920×1,080 pixels (1080i/1080p).

historical record Any document or artifact that is historically significant and is available to the public in an archive, library, government office, or digital repository. Compare to *public record*.

index An alphabetical list of topics or names with references to pages or sections in a larger document. An index is a tool intended to improve access and can appear in a paper or computerized format.

index term A field within a database defined as searchable.

informant See *interviewee*.

informed consent An agreement to do something or allow something to happen, made with complete knowledge of all relevant facts, such as the risks involved or any available alternatives. For example, an interviewer should inform the interviewee of all the potential uses of the interview, such as posting it on the Internet or depositing into an archive, and of the possible consequences above and beyond what is stated in the Legal Consent Form.

in-kind Support given in goods or services rather than cash.

insider/outsider Refers to the degree to which an individual belongs to, or is distant from, the community organization being studied.

intellectual property The area of law that regulates the ownership and use of creative works, including patent, copyright, and trademark. See also *copyright*.

interview A structured question and answer session between an interviewee and interviewer characterized by well-focused, clearly stated, open-ended, neutral questions aimed at gathering information not available from other sources. The interview is the basis for all oral history. See also *oral history, interviewee, interviewer*.

interviewee The person being interviewed. The person who has first-hand knowledge about the subject or topic of the interview and can effectively communicate this information.

interviewer The person who asks questions and guides the structure of an interview.

item level cataloging Cataloging system that describes each oral history as a single unit. This method of cataloging provides more detail than collection level cataloging and makes it easier to find information; however, it is much more time consuming. See also *collection level cataloging*.

lavaliere microphone Small dynamic microphone that clips on to the speaker's clothing.

legal consent form See *legal release agreement*.

legal release agreement The signed, legal agreement between the interviewee and the interviewer which clarifies a) intent (to conduct the interview), b) delivery and acceptance (of the interview itself to the designated party), c) copyright assignment (usually turned over to the interviewer or repository), and d) interviewee's rights to future use.

libel Written information that can damage a person's reputation. See also *slander, defamation*.

license A legal agreement granting one party certain permissions or rights without the right of ownership. Rights might include permission to use or re-use under specified circumstances.

life expectancy The length of time that an item is expected to remain intact and useful when kept in a typical repository or storage environment.

life interview An oral history interview that focuses on the life of one person, usually in a series of interviews. Many oral histories are a combination of life and topical interviews. See also *topical interview*.

local history The study of history in a geographically local context that often concentrates on the local community.

LOCKSS (Lots of Copies Keeps Stuff Safe) A simple preservation principle referring to the benefits of making multiple copies in multiple formats and storing them in multiple locations, as a means to preserve the content if one copy is destroyed.

machine dependent Any product that is dependent on a machine to be accessed. Audio and video recordings, and computerized record systems are machine dependent, whereas paper forms for records or paper transcripts are not.

management system A database system for keeping records for collections, projects, people, or online content. The system usually tracks tasks and objectives, with links to an inventory of materials processed and people involved in any capacity. A management system can be set up locally using a database or spreadsheet, or can be purchased as a commercial package. See also *collection management system*, *digital assets management system*.

MARC format (MAchine-Readable Cataloging) A *metdata* standard developed by the Library of Congress and adopted worldwide as the standard for library cataloging.

master recording An original recording that is preserved intact, as recorded.

matching funds Funds or in-kind goods or services supplied by a grant applicant in an amount that matches grant funds.

media independent Digital formats such as data files or streaming audio that are not dependent on a particular recording medium (CD, DVD). Media-independent digital content is stored and can be transported on a variety of media (e.g., CD-R, portable hard disk, and data tape), but this use of media is incidental to the content.

medium The physical device for capturing, storing, or preserving information. Examples: paper, discs, tape. The term format is often mistakenly used to describe these physical devices. Compare to *format*.

memory The ability to perceive, process, and recall information. Oral history is a methodology of recounting historical events through the memories of individuals. See also *false memory syndrome*.

memory card A solid-state digital storage device.

metadata Data about data. The sum total of information describing a resource, such as descriptive metadata entered by a cataloger; technical metadata generated by the computer; or administrative metadata concerning location of resource, access, and use privileges, entered by a curator. All the metadata is packaged in an "envelope" that travels with the digital resource throughout its life.

microphone A device that converts sound to electrical signals, usually for amplification. Although microphones can occur inside recorders, external microphones provide higher quality sound and should be used for oral history interviews. See also *directional microphone*, *omnidirectional microphone*, *dynamic/condenser microphone*, *stereo/mono microphone*.

migration See *data migration*.

more-product, less-process. A new concept in archival processing intended to address the almost universal backlog by making processing more efficient and getting archival collections into the hands of the users in a more timely fashion.

narrator See *interviewee*.

non-profit Organization that distributes funds for specifically defined goals rather than to shareholders. Also called not-for-profit.

obsolescence The loss of value or usefulness of an object even though it functions well. This can be due to outmoded equipment, inability to buy parts, newer technology, or a change in public taste.

omnidirectional microphone A microphone that picks up sound from any direction. Compare to *directional microphone*.

OPAC (Online Public Access Catalog) A library catalog whose records are in electronic format, stored and made accessible by way of a computer.

open format Published specification (format) for storing digital data, usually maintained by a standards organization, that can be used and implemented by anyone. See also *format*, *proprietary format*.

open source Computer application in which the source code is openly available. Open source applications are usually developed collaboratively.

oral history Primary source material collected in an interview setting with a witness to or a participant in an event or a way of life and grounded in context of time and place to give it meaning. Oral history is recorded for the purpose of preserving the information and making it available to others. The term refers to both the process and the final product.

oral history project A series of individual interviews with a number of interviewees focusing on one subject or event.

oral tradition A community's cultural and historical background preserved and passed on from one generation to the next in spoken stories and song, as distinct from a written tradition.

orphaned documents Documents in an archive that can't be made available to the public for any reason. Oral histories are often orphaned either because the proper Legal Release Agreement is missing, or because the equipment for listening to the interview is obsolete or unavailable.

outsource To contract with an independent agency for a task. A choice to outsource depends on the organization's collection, goals, and resources.

phantom power A method of providing power to condenser microphones by tapping into the power supply of the recording device it is attached to.

preservation Actions taken to stabilize and protect documents and artifacts from deteriorating, as well as retrospectively to treat or restore damaged documents. Preservation also includes the transfer of information to another medium.

preservation master The first copy made from a recorded interview. The original recording should be permanently stored in another location, and subsequent copies should be made from the preservation master. Compare to *user copy*.

primary source First-hand information with no interpretation between the document and the researcher. An oral history is a primary resource, as are diaries and letters. See also *secondary source*.

processing The steps taken to help make oral history interview information accessible to present and future users.

program An institutional based, ongoing undertaking for accomplishing specific goals. A program usually has ongoing funding and institutional support. Programs often support individual projects. Compare to *project*.

project A series of tasks to achieve a specific outcome within a specific time period. Most community oral history is organized into projects. Compare to *program*.

proprietary format A digital file format in which the source code is tightly held within a company or organization. See also *open format, format*.

public domain Used to describe creative works that are not subject to the copyright laws and may be used without permission of the creator or former rights holder. The work could either be expressly created for the public domain or the copyright limitation could have expired. Compare to *copyright*.

public history History that is seen, read, heard, or interpreted by a popular audience.

public record The full body of information available to the public through libraries, historical societies, government agencies, and the Internet.

Information can include books, journals, laws, and government documents. Information in the public record is the opposite of information which has restricted access for any reason. See also ***historical record***.

recording medium See ***medium***.

recording kit A customized "package" for audio or video recording equipment, which can include recorder, microphone, cables, and batteries.

re-grant To disperse funds received from another source.

release agreement See ***legal release agreement***.

repository A physical space with a long-term preservation plan for materials that go into the historical record. Libraries, archives, historical societies, museums, and digital repositories are examples of repositories.

restrictions Limitation imposed by the interviewee to legally restrict access to all or part of the interview content, for a limited time or permanently, for any reason. Though restrictions are discouraged both by interviewers and curators, sometimes they are unavoidable.

rights management The duties connected to intellectual property rights. Rights management for oral histories can include tracking restrictions and managing permission to use.

sampling rate The number of samples from a sound wave that the computer takes to make a digital file. The larger the sample the higher the quality of sound and the closer the digital sound represents the original.

scalability A criterion used to measure how well a procedure can be adapted to a much larger or a much smaller situation.

secondary source Interpretations of history based on the evidence contained in primary sources. Secondary sources involve generalization, analysis, synthesis, interpretation, or evaluation of the original information. *Primary* and *secondary* are relative terms, and some sources may be classified as primary or secondary, depending on the context. See also ***primary source***.

self-funded Describes an individual or organization that pays the full project cost without funding from outside sources.

server A computer that delivers a "service" to other computers in a network. Common servers are file (data) servers, print servers and mail servers.

service learning A method of teaching that combines formal instruction with a related service in the community.

slander Spoken information that can damage another person's reputation. See also ***libel***.

social tagging See *tagging*.

solid state Technology that uses data cards.

stereophonic/monophonic microphone A stereophonic microphone records sound from various sources on different channels. A monophonic microphone records all sounds on a single channel. Stereo microphones can also record as mono.

storage medium See *medium*.

streaming audio A method of transferring sound so it can be processed in a steady and continuous stream.

subject headings Descriptive terms pertaining to the item cataloged, based on a *controlled vocabulary*. Compare to *tagging*.

subsidy Financial assistance from a governmental unit or other source.

summary A recounting of the substance of an interview, highlighting the key points. It can vary in length from a paragraph to a few pages. An interview summary is sometimes created in addition to or instead a transcript.

tagging Also known as collaborative tagging, folksonomy, or social tagging, this is a method for customizing and enhancing online retrieval whereby users add keywords to an information resource. These tags are indexed and available to further users for retrieval. Compare to *subject headings*, *controlled vocabulary*.

thesaurus A list of terms and concepts, usually dealing with a specific discipline, that provides a standardized vocabulary to use in searching a database. See also *controlled vocabulary*.

topical interview An interview conducted with the purpose to elicit personal accounts of a particular event, place, occupation, or other specific topic. See also *life interview*.

transcript A verbatim version of the spoken word. A transcript matches the interview as closely as possible and contains the full and accurately spelled names of all persons and places mentioned in the interview.

uncompressed See *data compression*.

user copy Third generation copy of an audio or video recording, made for public use. Compare to *preservation master*.

video A method of capturing, recording, processing, transmitting, and reconstructing moving images using film, electronic signals, or digital media.

visual history A recorded oral history interview using video instead of audio.

volunteer Work without compensation.

RESOURCES

These resources will be useful to community oral historians throughout the life cycle of an of an oral history project. Resources include articles and books in print and in electronic formats; pointers to organizations and online discussion groups; examples of project manuals and presentations of community history; and several technical reports to support planning and fundraising.

Top Ten

Here are the top choices for a well-rounded compilation of oral history resources.

• Baylor University Institute for Oral History. *Style Guide: a Quick Reference for Editing Oral Memoirs*. Rev. 2005. *http://www.baylor.edu/content/services/document.php?id=14142*. A popular resource among oral historians for transcribing and editing interviews.

• H-Oralhist (Online Community). *http://www.h-net.org/~oralhist/*. The best source for asking practical questions and keeping up to date on all aspects of oral history. All discussions are archived and searchable from this homepage.

• Neuenschwander, John A. *A Guide to Oral History and the Law*. New York: Oxford University Press, 2009. The definitive guide to legal issues in oral history. Neuenschwander, a lawyer, judge, and oral historian, has been writing about oral history and the law for many years.

• Oral History in the Digital Age (OHDA) (Online Community). http://ohda.matrix.msu.edu/. OHDA grew out of an IMLS funded project bringing together experts to re-examine the field in the digital age. The results of these discussions and their follow-up should inform the profession in the 21st century.

• Oral History Association (OHA). http://www.oralhistory.org/. The oral history professional association for the United States. Hosts an active website, newsletter, peer reviewed journal, *Oral History Review*, and an annual conference. In particular, note the *Principles and Best Practices*, the professional standards adopted by the organization in 2009.

- Ritchie, Donald A. *Doing Oral History.* 2nd ed. New York: Oxford University Press, 2003. A comprehensive overview of the field, written in question–and-answer format. Extensive resource list.

- Schneider, William. *So They Understand: Cultural Issues in Oral History.* Logan, UT: Utah State University Press, 2002. This text deals with the complex issues encountered when doing oral history within a specific cultural context.

- Sommer, Barbara W. and Mary Kay Quinlan. *The Oral History Manual.* 2nd ed. Lanham, MD: AltaMira Press, 2009. A step–by-step guide for doing oral history used as a college and university text as well as by historical organizations, public historians, and community oral historians.

- Yow, Valerie Raleigh. *Recording Oral History: a Guide for the Humanities and Social Sciences.* Walnut Creek, CA: AltaMira Press, 2005. The author, a psychotherapist and oral historian, provides a balanced guide to the oral history process with an emphasis on the oral history interview.

- Zusman, Angela. *Story Bridges: a Guide to Conducting Intergenerational Oral History Projects.* Walnut Creek, CA: Left Coast Press, Inc., 2010. A guide to planning and conducting an oral history project, with an emphasis on intergenerational oral history.

Organizations

Networking is the best way to find your way into a new field. In addition to the resources offered by these national and international organizations, be sure to seek out organizations within your own community or region.

American Association of Museums (AAM). http://www.aam-us.org/. Hosts an annual conference, publications, and an accreditation program.

American Association of State and Local History (AASLH). http://www.aaslh. org. Supports state and local historians through professional development, publications, an annual conference, and a code of professional standards.

American Library Association (ALA). http://ala.org/. The professional home for the vast network of libraries in the United States, with an emphasis on public libraries. Sponsors an annual conference, special interest groups, research, and grants and serves as a political lobbying body.

Association of Moving Image Archivists (AMIA). http://www.amianet.org/. A non-profit association for archivists working with film and video. Offers an online discussion group, an annual conference, and a journal, *The Moving Image*.

Association for Recorded Sound Collections (ARSC). http://www.arsc-audio.org/.
Dedicated to the preservation and study of sound recordings in all genres,
in all formats, and from all periods. ARSC sponsors an annual conference,
professional development opportunities, and an online discussion group and
publishes the *ARSC Journal*.

Groundswell: Oral History for Social Change. http://www.oralhistoryforsocialchange.
org/. Network of community activists and oral historians working for social
change, offering educational and networking opportunities and tools for working
within your own community.

Heritage Preservation. http://www.heritagepreservation.org/. Non-profit
organization dedicated to helping museums, libraries, and historical societies
preserve American cultural heritage. Includes print and online reports, and
curriculum materials.

Institute of Museum and Library Services (IMLS). www.imls.gov. An independent
federal agency supporting museums and libraries of all types including
public, academic, research, special and tribal, and the full range of museums
including art, history, science and technology, children's museums, historical
societies, tribal museums, planetariums,botanic gardens and zoos.

International Association of Sound and Audiovisual Archives (IASA). http://www.
iasa-web.org/. Interdisciplinary, international organization devoted to the
preservation of recorded sound and audiovisual documents. Publishes a journal
and a newsletter, hosts an annual conference, and offers grants for research.

International Oral History Association (IOHA). http://iohanet.org/. Supports
oral history around the world with a biennial conference, a journal, *Words
and Silences,* available free online, and a newsletter. Many countries have
oral history associations including United States, England, Canada, Brazil,
Argentina, Mexico, Australia, and New Zealand.

National Archives and Records Administration (NARA). http://www.archives.
gov. The seat of the United States government archives, NARA is the umbrella
for the network of US government archives, as well as an excellent starting
point for historical research. Includes publications, online resources, and
workshops. The National Historical Publication and Records Commission
(NHPRC) is its grantsmaking affiliate.

National Council on Public History (NCPH). http://www.ncph.org. Professional
association for public historians from a variety of disciplines. Offers an
annual conference, sponsors H-Public online discussion forum, a peer
reviewed journal, *The Public Historian*, and professional development
opportunities.

Online Audiovisual Catalogers (OLAC). http://olacinc.org/. American Library
Association affiliate devoted to the cataloging of non-print media, including
oral histories in audio, visual, and electronic formats. Hosts an annual
conference, online discussion group, and publications.

Oral History Association (OHA). http://www.oralhistory.org/. The professional association for oral historians. Hosts an annual conference, an online discussion forum, H-Oralhist, professional development opportunities, and best practices. There are a number of regional oral history associations, including Michigan, Midwest, New England, Northwest US, Mid-Atlantic United States, Southwest United States, and Texas.

Organization of American Historians (OAH). http://www.oah.org. Promotes the study of American history through a conference–a peer reviewed journal, *Journal of American History,* and curriculum resources.

Small Museum Association (SMA). http://www.smallmuseum.org/. Though it primarily serves the mid-Atlantic region of the United States, SMA meets a need as a networking portal for smaller organizations, including an annual conference.

Society of American Archivists (SAA). http://www2.archivists.org/. Serves the archives profession through an annual conference, online discussion forum, a journal entitled *The American Archivist,* related publications, and professional development opportunities. Includes a special interest group for oral history. The website has an extensive list of local, state, and national archival organizations. See http://www.archivists.org/assoc-orgs/directory/index.asp.

Oral History Programs

Many existing oral history programs are eager to partner with community projects or to host the completed oral histories in their associated repositories. Most programs prefer to be contacted before the project begins in order to work together throughout the project.

Alaska. Oral History Program. Elmer E. Rasmuson Library, University of Alaska, Fairbanks. http://library.uaf.edu/oral-history.

California, San Francisco Bay Area. Regional Oral History Office (ROHO). University of California, Berkeley. http://bancroft.berkeley.edu/ROHO/. Offers a summer training workshop.

California, Southern. Center for Oral and Public History. California State University, Fullerton. http://coph.fullerton.edu/.

California, Southern. UCLA Oral History Research Center. Los Angeles. http://oralhistory.library.ucla.edu/.

Colorado. Maria Rogers Oral History Program. Carnegie Branch, Boulder Public Library, Boulder. http://boulderlibrary.org/carnegie/collections/mrohp.html.

Kentucky. Louie B. Nunn Center for Oral History. University of Kentucky, Lexington. http://libraries.uky.edu/nunncenter.

Minnesota. Minnesota Historical Society. http://www.mnhs.org/people/mngg/ stories/oralhistory.htm.

New York. Columbia Center for Oral History (CCOH). Columbia University, New York. http://library.columbia.edu/indiv/ccoh.html. Offers a summer training workshop.

Nevada. Oral History Research Center. University of Nevada, Las Vegas. http:// library.nevada.edu/oral_histories/index.html.

North Carolina. Southern Oral History Program. University of North Carolina, Chapel Hill. http://www.sohp.org/.

Oklahoma. Oral History Research Program. Oklahoma State University, Stillwater. http://www.library.okstate.edu/oralhistory/.

Texas. Baylor University Institute for Oral History. Baylor University, Waco. http:// www.baylor.edu/oralhistory/.

Washington, DC. Veterans History Project (Library of Congress). http://www.loc. gov/vets/. Accepts oral histories from any US veteran.

Wisconsin. UW Madison Oral History Program. University of Wisconsin, Madison. http://archives.library.wisc.edu/oral-history/overview.html.

Project Manuals

These manuals are written for specific projects, programs, or audiences. All are good examples of how a community oral history project might approach training and project documentation.

Baylor University Institute for Oral History. *Workshop on the Web.* http://www. baylor.edu/oralhistory/index.php?id=23560. Viewed 5/6/2012. A series of useful online tutorials including Introduction to Oral history, Digital Oral History Workshop, Teaching and Learning Oral History, Transcribing Style Guide, The Heart of Oral History: How to Interview, and Organizing oral history projects.

Handbook for Oral History in the National Park Service (Draft). 2005. http://www. cr.nps.gov/history/oh/oral.htm.

Hunt, Marjorie. *Smithsonian Folklife and Oral History Interview Guide.* Washington, DC: Smithsonian Center for Folklife and Cultural Heritage, 2012. http://www.storiesfrommainstreet.org/education/Smithsonian_Oral_ History_Guide.pdf.

Mediavilla, Cindy. *California Stories Uncovered: Conducting Oral History Interviews: a How-to Manual.* California Council for the Humanities, n.d. http://www.calhum.org/files/uploads/other/oral_history_manual.pdf.

Oral History: A Practical Guide. 4th ed. Chapel Hill, NC: Southern Oral History Program, University of North Carolina, 2005. http://www.ibiblio.org/sohp/howto/guide/index.html.

Oral History Project Guidelines. St. Paul, MN: Minnesota Historical Society. Oral History Office, 2001. http://www.mnhs.org/collections/oralhistory/ohguidelines.pdf.

PATHWAYS: Discovering Your Connections to History. A Project of the American Association for State and Local History, 2002, http://www.aaslh.org/pathways.htm. A three-volume programming guide for public historians; includes programming guide for public historians; includes several sections on doing and using oral history.

Sommer, Barbara W., Mary Kay Quinlan, and Paul Eisloeffel. *Capturing the Living Past: an Oral History Primer.* Lincoln, NE: Nebraska State Historical Society, 2005. http://www.nebraskahistory.org/lib-arch/research/audiovis/oral_history/.

Truesdell, Barbara. *Oral History Techniques: How to Organize and Conduct Oral History Interviews.* Indiana University Center for the Study of History and Memory, n.d. http://www.indiana.edu/~cshm/oral_history_techniques.pdf.

Professional Standards and Best Practices

Professional and ethical guidelines underpin every successful community oral history project. The guidelines established by these organizations offer examples of professional standards of conduct in a variety of disciplines and can be applied to in oral history.

Alaska Native Knowledge Network. *Guidelines for respecting cultural knowledge.* Adopted 2000. http://www.ankn.uaf.edu/publications/Knowledge.pdf.

American Anthropological Association. *Statements on ethics.* Rev. 1998. http://www.aaanet.org/committees/ethics/ethicscode.pdf.

American Association of Museums. *Code of ethics for museums.* Rev. 2000. http://aam-us.org/museumresources/ethics/upload/Code-of-Ethics-for-Museums.pdf.

American Association of State and Local History. *Statement of professional standards and ethics.* Adopted 2002. http://www.aaslh.org/ethics.htm.

American Historical Association. *Statement on Standards of Professional Conduct.* Updated 2011. http://www.historians.org/pubs/Free/ProfessionalStandards.cfm.

American Library Association. *Code of Ethics. Rev. 2008. http://www.ala.org/advocacy/proethics/codeofethics/codeethics.*

National Council on Public History. *NCPH Code of Ethics and Professional Conduct.* Adopted 2007. http://ncph.org/cms/about/bylaws-and-ethics/.

Oral History Association. *Principles and Best Practices.* Updated 2009. http://www.oralhistory.org/do-oral-history/principles-and-practices.

Society of American Archivists. *Core Values Statement and Code of Ethics.* Approved 2011 and 2012. http://www2.archivists.org/statements/saa-core-values-statement-and-code-of-ethics.

Community Oral History in General

The American Archivist. (1938-) http://www2.archivists.org/american-archivist. Peer reviewed journal of the Society of American Archivist. Available online for free except for the most recent six issues.

Burke, Peter. *Varieties of Cultural History.* Ithaca, NY: Cornell University Press, 1997. Of special interest is Chapter 2. "History of Social Memory."

Center for History and New Media (CHNM), George Mason University, Fairfax, VA. (Institution) http://chnm.gmu.edu. Supports projects which use digital technology to bring history to a wide audience. The website offers technology tools for the humanities.

Centre for Oral History and Digital Storytelling, Concordia University, Montreal, Quebec. (Institution) http://storytelling.concordia.ca/oralhistory/.

Dunaway, David K. and Willa K. Baum, eds. *Oral History: An Interdisciplinary Reader*, 2nd ed. Thousand Oaks, CA: AltaMira Press, 1996.

Freund, Alexander. "Oral History as Process Generated Data." *Historical Social Research* 34, no. 1. (2009): 22-48.

Frisch, Michael. *A Shared Authority: Essays on the Craft and Meaning of Oral and Public History.* Albany: SUNY Press, 1991. This classic work has helped to define the field. Any works by Frisch are worth reading.

Gardner, James B., and Peter S. LaPaglia. *Public History: Essays from the Field.* Malabar, FL: Krieger Pub. Co., 1999.

H-Net (Online Community). http://www.h-net.org/. A consortium of online discussion groups devoted to the humanities, including H-Oralhist (oral history), H-Museum (museum studies), H-Local (local history) and H-Public (public history). Postings include funding opportunities, conferences, new publications, and serious discussions on current topics.

History@Work (Blog). http://publichistorycommons.org/. Sponsored by the National Council on Public History.

Kammen, Carol. *On Doing Local History.* 2nd ed. Walnut Creek, CA: AltaMira Press, 2003.

Kyvig, David and Myron A. Marty. *Nearby History: Exploring the Past around You.* 3rd ed. Lanham, MD: AltaMira Press, 2010.

Journal of American History (JAH). (1964-) Journal for the Organization of American Historians.

Linehan, Andy, ed. *Aural History: Essays on Recorded Sound.* London: British Library, National Sound Archive, 2001. Book includes CD with sound samples. Of particular interest to community oral historians is Robert Perks "The Century Speaks: a Millennium Oral History Project," pp. 27–40.

MATRIX (Center for Humane Arts, Letters, and Social Sciences Online). http://www2.matrix.msu.edu. This Michigan State University based institute is devoted to the application of new technologies for teaching, research, and outreach. Creates and maintains online resources, provides training in computing and new teaching technologies, and creates forums for the exchange of ideas and expertise in the field.

Oral History (1969-) Journal of the United Kingdom Oral History Society.

Oral History Forum d'histoire oral, formerly *Canadian Oral History Association Journal* (1975/6-) Journal of the Canadian Oral History Association.

Oral History Review (1973-). Journal of the Oral History Association (US). Includes articles, interviews, review essays, and book and media reviews related to the practice of oral history in a variety of settings and the use and interpretation of interviews for a variety of scholarly and public purposes.

Perks, Robert, and Alistair Thomson, eds. *The Oral History Reader.* 2nd ed. New York: Routledge, 2006. Anthology of previously published work on the more theoretical aspects of oral history.

Portelli, Alessandro. *The Battle of Valle Giulia: Oral History and the Art of Dialogue.* Madison: University of Wisconsin Press, 1997. Elegantly written essays on the interview, with case studies focusing on interviews about war and about political movements. Any works by Portelli are worth reading.

The Public Historian (1978-). Journal of the National Council for Public History.

Ritchie, Donald A., ed. *Oxford Handbook of Oral History.* New York: Oxford University Press, 2010. Articles by 40 authors on five continents on every aspect of oral history in the 21st century.

Rosenzweig, Roy and David Thelen. *The Presence of the Past: Popular Uses of History in American Life.* New York: Columbia University Press, 2000. The authors interviewed 1,500 Americans about their connection to the past and how it influences their daily lives and hopes for the future. Similar surveys have been done in Australia (*History and the Crossroads: Australians and the Past,* by Paul Ashton and Paula Hamilton, 2010) and Canada (*Canadians and the Past*).

Rosenzweig, Roy, Susan Porter Benson and Stephen Brier. *Presenting the Past: Essays on History and the Public.* Philadelphia: Temple University Press, 1986. One of the first treatments of public history when it was emerging as a field.

Schneider, William. *So They Understand: Cultural Issues in Oral History*. Logan, UT: Utah State University Press, 2002.

Thompson, Paul. *The Voice of the Past: Oral History*, 3rd ed. New York: Oxford Press, 2000.

Yow, Valerie Raleigh. *Recording Oral History: A Guide for the Humanities and Social Sciences*. 2nd ed. Walnut Creek, CA: AltaMira Press, 2005. A solid discussion of project planning, interview methodology, and the use and interpretation of oral history materials.

Community

Archibald, Robert R. *A Place to Remember: Using History to Build Community*. Walnut Creek: AltaMira Press, 1999.

Diaz, Rose T. and Andrew B. Russell. "Oral Historians: Community Oral History and the Cooperative Ideal." In *Public History: Essays from the Field*, edited by James B. Gardner and Peter S. LaPaglia. Rev. ed. Malabar, FL: Krieger Publishing Company, 2004.

Hamilton, Paula and Linda Shopes. *Oral History and Public Memories*. Philadelphia: Temple University Press, 2008.

Hardy, Charles, III. "A People's History of Industrial Philadelphia: Reflections on Community Oral History Projects and the Uses of the Past." *Oral History Review,* 2006. 33: 1-32.

Mercier, Laurie and Buckendorf, Madeline. *Using Oral History in Community History Projects*. Carlisle, PA: Oral History Association, 2010.

Olson, Karin. *Essentials of Qualitative Interviewing*. Walnut Creek, CA: Left Coast Press, Inc., 2011.

Schneider, William. *Living with Stories: Telling, Re-telling and Remembering*. Logan, UT: Utah State University Press, 2008.

Schneider, William. *So They Understand: Cultural Issues in Oral History*. Logan, UT: Utah State University Press, 2002.

Shopes, Linda. "Oral History and the Study of Communities: Problems, Paradoxes, and Possibilities." *The Journal of American History* 89: 2 (September 2002): 588-598.

Project Administration

American Association for State and Local History. *Standards and Excellence Program for History Organizations (StEPS)*, 2010. http://www.aaslh.org/steps.htm. This self-administered assessment program will help small and medium-sized history organizations evaluate policies and practices within six categories developed by AASLH.

American Association for State and Local History. *Technical Leaflet Series*. http://www.aaslh.org/leaflets.htm. Short leaflets on topics of interest to public historians. Recent topics include copyright and licensing issues for digital collections (#251), the importance of community history (#252), and preparing an organization for attracting grants (#257).

Baum, Willa K. *Oral History for the Local Historical Society*. 3rd ed. Walnut Creek, CA: AltaMira Press, 1995. An older title that stands the test of time.

DeBlasio, Donna M., Charles F. Ganzert, David H. Mould, Stephen H. Paschen, Howard L. Sacks. *Catching Stories: a Practical Guide to Oral History*. Athens, OH: University of Ohio Press, 2009.

Johnson, Larry, Holly Witchey, and Keene Haywood. *The 2010 Horizon Report: Museum Edition*. Austin, TX: The New Media Consortium, 2010. http://www.nmc.org/pdf/2010-Horizon-Report-Museum.pdf. This report, produced by an international panel of museum, education, and technology experts focuses on technology within a context of museum education and interpretation.

H-Net (Online community), Interdisciplinary network of scholars, educators, and activists is an excellent source for current information. http://www.h-net.org/. These forums are of particular interest to community oral historians:

H-Local. Local history. http://www.h-net.org/~local/.

H-Museum. Museum studies. http://www.h-net.org/~museum/.

H-Oralhist. Oral History. http://www.h-net.org/~oralhist/.

H-Public. Public history. http://www.h-net.org/~public/.

Neuenschwander, John A. *A Guide to Oral History and the Law*. New York: Oxford University Press, 2009. Definitive guide to legal aspects in oral history.

The Public Historian. The journal of the National Council for Public History.

Sommer, Barbara W. and Mary Kay Quinlan. *The Oral History Manual*. 2nd ed. Lanham, MD: AltaMira Press, 2009.

Trimble, Charles E., Barbara W. Sommer, and Mary Kay Quinlan. *The American Indian Oral History Manual: Making Many Voices Heard*. Walnut Creek, CA: Left Coast Press, Inc., 2008.

Whitman, Glenn. *Dialogue with the Past: Engaging Students & Meeting Standards through Oral History*. Walnut Creek, CA: AltaMira Press, 2004.

Zusman, Angela. *Story Bridges: a Guide to Conducting Intergenerational Oral History Projects*. Walnut Creek, CA: Left Coast Press, Inc., 2010.

Fundraising and Networking

Brophy, Sarah S. *Is Your Museum Grant-Ready? Assess Your Organizations Potential for Funding*. Lanham, MD: AltaMira Press, 2005.

Geever, Jane. *The Foundation Center's Guide to Proposal Writing.* 5th ed. New York: The Foundation Center, 2007.

Institute of Museum and Library Services (IMLS). www.imls.gov. Independent federal grant making agency which administers Library Services and Technology Act (LSTA) grants to libraries and museums. Funds large projects, including oral history.

MATRIX (Center for Human Arts, Letters, and Social Sciences Online). http://www2.matrix.msu.edu. Devoted to the application of new technologies for teaching, research, and outreach. Works with communities to turn ideas into fundable projects.

National Endowment for the Humanities (NEH). http://www.neh.gov/. The federal government body that issues large grants in the humanities.

New Media Consortium (NMC). http://www.nmc.org/. Consortium of universities, museums, and research centers, devoted to exploring new media and technologies in the humanities. Services include research, publications, a blog, and a conference.

State Humanities Councils are often the first place for a community oral history project to seek funding. All states have humanities councils and most are friendly to community initiated projects. NEH provides a directory: http://www.neh.gov/about/state-humanities-councils.

Recording Technology

Because recording technology changes so rapidly, the Internet is the best source for current practice. The websites in this section are commonly used in the oral history field for up-to-date, trustworthy information.

Digital recording: here to stay. Boston, MA: Tape Transcription Center, 2006. http://www.ttctranscriptions.com/Digitalvsanalog.html. Viewed 7/26/2012. A good comparison of audio versus digital formats.

DigitalOmnium: Oral History, Archives, and Digital Technology. http://digitalomnium.com/. Viewed 7/26/2012. Oral historian Doug Boyd's personal blog. Frequent articles and updates on technology for oral historians in the areas of recording, archiving, and preservation.

Kovolos, Andy. *Digital Audio Field Recording Equipment Guide.* Middlebury, VT: Vermont Folklife Center. Frequent updates. http://www.vermontfolklifecenter.org/archive/res_audioequip.htm. Viewed 7/26/2012. The latest information on audio technology specifically for oral historians.

Morton, David L. *Sound Recording: the Life Story of a Technology.* Baltimore, MD: Johns Hopkins University Press, 2006. Mortin is a new media expert and writer. An online companion timeline is available at http://www.recording-history.org/.

Schoenherr, Steve. *Recording Technology History.* (2005). http://homepage.mac.com/oldtownman/recording/notes.html#origins. Timeline for recording technology, compiled by retired history professor Steve Schoenheer.

Transom.org. (Blog). http://transom.org/. Viewed 7/26/2012. This public radio blog has many technology discussions and tools useful to oral historians.

Wikipedia has a variety of up-to-date articles with helpful links on recording technology. http://en.wikipedia.org/wiki/Main_Page.

After the Interview in General

AMIA-L (Online forum). http://www.amianet.org/participate/listserv.php. Useful resource for processing and cataloging video interviews.

ARSC recorded round discussion list (Online forum). http://www.arsc-audio.org/arsclist.html. A network for sound preservationists. Includes information useful to preservation of oral histories.

Brown, Michael F. "Can culture be copyrighted?" *Current Anthropology.* 39, no. 2 (April 1998): 193–222.

Behrnd-Klod, Menzi L. and Peter J. Wosh. *Privacy & Confidentiality Perspectives: Archivists and Archival Records.* Chicago: Alpha Publishing House, Society of American Archivists, 2009.

Council on Library and Information Resources (CLIR). http://www.clir.org/. An independent, nonprofit organization with a strong research and publication arm. Collaborates with libraries, cultural institutions, and communities of higher learning.

A Guide to Deeds of Gift. Chicago: Society of American Archivists, 1998. http://www.archivists.org/publications/deed_of_gift.asp.

Hunter, Gregory S. *Developing and Maintaining Practical Archives: a How-To-Do-It Manual.* 2nd ed. New York: Neal-Schuman, 2003.

Lipinski, Thomas A., ed. *Libraries, Museums and Archives: Legal Issues and Ethical Challenges in the New Information Age.* Lanham, MD: Scarecrow Press, 2002.

MacKay, Nancy. *Curating Oral Histories.* Walnut Creek, CA: Left Coast Press. Inc., 2007. The definitive work on processing, cataloging, and preservation of oral histories.

Pearce-Moses, Richard. *Glossary of Archival and Records Terminology.* Chicago: Society of American Archivists, 2005. Also online at http://www.archivists.org/glossary/.

Report on orphan works. Washington, DC: United States Copyright Office, Library of Congress, 2006. http://www.copyright.gov/orphan/orphan-report-full.pdf.

Stim, Richard. *Getting Permission: How to License & Clear Copyrighted Materials Online & Off.* 4th ed. Berkeley, CA: Nolo Press, 2010.

Swain, Ellen D. "Oral history in the Archives: Its Documentary Role in the Twenty-first Century," *American Archivist*, v. 66 (Spring/summer 2003): 139-158. Reprinted in Perks and Thomson. *The Oral History Reader*. 2nd ed. New York: Routledge, 2006. History of archiving oral histories, literature review and overview of the issues involved.

Yakel, Elizabeth. *Starting an Archives.* Chicago: Society of American Archivists, Scarecrow Press, 1994.

Transcribing and Editing

Dudding, Michael. *Abstracting Oral Histories (A How-To Guide).* http://www.oralhistory.org.nz/documents/duddingabstractingguide2008.pdf. An excellent model for creating timed interview summary as an alternative to a full transcript.

Frisch, Michael. "Oral history and the digital revolution: toward a post-documentary sensibility." In *The Oral History Reader*. 2nd ed., Robert Perks and Alistair Thomson, eds. London: Routledge, 2006. Presents the case against transcribing.

Klemmer, Scott R., Jamey Graham, Gregory J. Wolff, et al. "Books with Voices: Paper Transcripts as a Physical Interface to Oral Histories." In [Scott R. Klemmer, Jamey Graham, Gregory J. Wolff, James A. Landay.] Proceedings of the SIGCHI Conference on Human Factors in Computer Systems, 2003. 89–96.

Powers, Willow Roberts. *Transcription Techniques for the Spoken Word.* Walnut Creek, CA: AltaMira Press, 2005.

Shopes, Linda. "Editing Oral History for Publication." *Oral History Forum d'histoire orale* 31 (2011). 1–24. This paper is the best presentation of the possibilities for digital technologies for oral history access.

Wilmsen, Carl. "For the Record: Editing and the Production of Meaning in Oral History." *Oral History Review*. 28:1 (Winter 2001).

Transcription Software

Express-scribe transcription playback software. (NCH Swift Sound). http://www.nch.com.au/scribe.

Start-stop dictation and transcription systems. (HTH Engineering). http://www.startstop.com/.

Transcribing and Editing Guides

Style Guide: a Quick Guide for Editing Oral Memoirs. http://www.baylor.edu/
content/services/document.php?id=14142. Waco, TX: Baylor University
Institute for Oral History, 2007.

Transcribing, Editing and Processing Oral Histories. http://www.mnhs.org/
collections/oralhistory/ohtranscribing.pdf. St. Paul, MN: Minnesota
Historical Society Oral History Office, 2001.

Cataloging and Metadata

AUTOCAT (Online discussion group). http://www.cwu.edu/~dcc/Autocat-
ToC-2007.html. A semi-moderated discussion list serving the international
cataloging community.

*IASA Cataloguing Rules: a Manual for the Description of Sound Recordings and
Related Audiovisual Media,* compiled and edited by the IASA Editorial Group
convened by Mary Miliano. Stockholm: IASAA, 1999. http://www.iasa-web.
org/iasa-cataloguing-rules.

Library of Congress. *MARC Standards.* http://www.loc.gov/marc/. Currently, the
internationally recognized content standard for cataloging.

Oral History Metadata Synchronizer (OHMS). An open source tool for large oral
history collections, which automates metadata creation, developed at the
University of Kentucky. Plans include an implementation for OHMS that can
work as a plug-in with CONTENTdm, OMEKA, KORA, and Drupal.

OLAC Electronic Discussion List (Online discussion group). http://olacinc.org/.
Internet and AV Media catalogers' network.

Voice Preserve. http://voicepreserve.org/. A model for a digital repository for
the voice. Using Voice Preserve's guidelines and templates, community oral
historians can contribute oral histories directly to the repository.

Preservation

Connecting to Collections Online Community. http://www.connectingtocollections.
org/. An online meeting spot for smaller museums, libraries, archives, and
historical societies to get answers to collections care questions and quickly locate
reliable preservation resources and to help curators network with colleagues.

Conservation Online: Resources for Conservation Professionals. (CoOL). http://
palimpsest.stanford.edu. Web portal for conservation and preservation, hosted
by Stanford University.

The Field Audio Collection Evaluation Tool (FACET) is a points-based tool for ranking field collections for the level of deterioration they exhibit and the amount of risk they carry. This tool helps collection managers construct a prioritized list of collections by the level of risk they represent, enabling informed selection for preservation. Combining FACET with a process that assesses research value provides strong justification for preservation dollars. FACET was developed by Mike Casey at the Archives of Traditional Music, Indiana University. micasey@indiana.edu. Not available yet

Folk Heritage Collections in Crisis. Washington, DC: CLIR, 2001. http://www.clir.org/pubs/reports/pub96/contents.html. Still relevant to oral history curators, this study highlights the vulnerability of audio and visual materials in archives.

IASA Technical Committee. *Guidelines on the Production and Preservation of Digital Audio Objects*, ed. by Kevin Bradley. 2nd ed. 2009. (Standards, Recommended Practices and Strategies, IASA-TC 04). www.iasa-web.org/tc04/audio-preservation.

IASA Technical Committee. *The Safeguarding of the Audio Heritage: Ethics, Principles and Preservation Strategy*, ed. by Dietrich Schüller. Version 3, 2005 (Standards, Recommended Practices and Strategies, (IASA-TC 03).

International Association of Sound and Audiovisual Archives. www.iasa-web.org/tc03/ethics-principles-preservation-strategy.

Library of Congress Preservation Portal. http://www.loc.gov/preservation/. A compendium of resources for preservation, including funding opportunities. A separate portal for digital preservation at http://www.digitalpreservation.gov.

LOCKSS (Lots of Copies Keeps Stuff Safe). http://www.lockss.org/. Open source software for libraries and archives for preserving and providing access to digital collections.

National Endowment for the Humanities, Division of Preservation and Access. http://www.neh.gov/divisions/preservation. Offers grants to archives and oral history repositories.

Northeast Document Conservation Center. http://www.nedcc.org/home.php. A non-profit organization devoted to conservation and preservation of archival materials. Offers consultations, workshops, and publications.

The Signal: Digital Preservation (Blog) http://blogs.loc.gov/digitalpreservation/. Very informative blog on preservation issues, from the Library of Congress.

Smith, Abby, David Randal Allen and Karen Allen. *Survey of the State of Audio Collections in Academic Libraries.* Washington, DC: CLIR, 2004. http://www.clir.org/pubs/reports/pub128/contents.html

Sound Directions: Digital Preservation and Access for Global Audio Heritage. Updated 2008. http://www.dlib.indiana.edu/projects/sounddirections/. A joint initiative of Indiana University Archives of Traditional Music and Harvard University's Archive of World Music. Includes best practices for audio preservation.

Washington State Library. *Digital Best Practices.* http://digitalwa.statelib.wa.gov/ newsite/best.htm.

Oral Histories on the Internet

Cohen, Daniel J. and Roy Rosenzweig. *Digital History: a Guide to Gathering, Preserving and Presenting the Past on the Web.* Philadelphia: University of Pennsylvania Press, 2006. Free electronic version at http://chnm.gmu.edu/ digitalhistory/. Also available in print.

EuScreen. *Online Access to AudioVisual Heritage.* Status Report 1, January 2011, Status Report 2, July 2012. Search report name at http://pro.europeana.eu/. Though these reports survey online access to television in Europe, insightful observations can apply to online access to oral history as well.

A Framework of Guidance for Building Good Digital Collections. 3rd ed. NISO, 2008. http://framework.niso.org/.

A

abstracts of interviews, III:127, V:69,
V:155n.9

academic research centers
differences with projects originating
in, I:10, II:10, III:10, IV:10,
V:14
early projects of, I:20–21
as repositories, I:37

access
cataloging enables, V:73
community, I:64–65, V:100–101
confidentiality issues and, III:65,
III:79
defining, III:124, V:92, V:99
direct vs. indirect, V:71–72
to equipment storage space, III:65
establishing historical context for
future, I:56–57
future technology and, I:54–55,
II:101
as goal of processing, V:26
managing, III:132–33
preservation and, III:87, V:93, V:98
as purpose of project, I:45–46
repositories and, I:47, III:132,
III:133, V:93, V:156n.12
user-friendliness of transcripts,
V:56, V:57
video issues, I:41, I:42
to work space, II:76

See also Internet, access on; Legal
Release Agreement; Legal
Release Agreement (Restric-
tions); repositories

accountants, III:54

accuracy, V:40, V:57

acknowledgements
at end of project, V:54, V:105, V:108
importance of frequent, III:64
planning for, II:102
recipients, II:34
types of, III:64

Advent House Ministries project in
Michigan, III:135–36

advisory committees/boards, community
supporters on, II:34

advocacy, as overt purpose of project,
IV:28

after-the-interview tasks. *See* cataloging;
entries beginning with *transcri;*
post-interview tasks; processing

announcements, V:105

anonymity of interviewees, I:27

Arapahoe County, Colorado 2008 election project, I:29–30

archives
building community, V:110
cataloging model, V:75–76
data files storage and maintenance
by, III:85
for future availability, I:13, II:13,
III:13, IV:13, V:17

online, V:27
planning, II:92
as repositories, II:66, V:93, V:94
arguments, refraining from, IV:31
Arlington, VA Halls High View Park
    Archive Project, V:110
Arrowhead Civilian Conservation Corps
    Documentation Project, 136
art as memory aids, I:17
artifacts, IV:98–100, IV:107
audio media
    delivery of, V:63
    labeling, V:41–42
    overview of post-interview tasks,
        V:50
    as preservation format, V:96
    time-coded indexes, V:69, V:126
    transcribing from, V:62
audio recording equipment
    budgeting for, II:92
    choosing, II:78–80, II:82–83, III:83
    data format for, IV:62
    ethical considerations and, I:54
    final check, IV:79–80
    set-up at interview location of, IV:76
    standards, II:119–20, II:122
    See also microphones
audit-checking, V:63
audits, as grant requirement, III:97
authorship, II:35–36, II:37

B
Bancroft, Hubert Howe, I:20
bartering, obtaining donations by, III:98
Becker, Susan, III:129, V:117
before-the-interview tasks of interviewers
    background knowledge about topic,
        IV:63–64
    checking interviewing kits, IV:76
    development of interview outline,
        IV:67–72
    ethical considerations, IV:28–30
    familiarization with project goals,
        IV:60
    final equipment check, IV:79–80
    interviewee-specific research,
        IV:64–65

at interview location, IV:76–78
overview of, IV:19, IV:60
record keeping, IV:72, IV:74
restrictions on interviews, V:28
training, importance of, I:13, I:63,
    II:13, III:13, III:50, IV:13,
    IV:51, V:17
training duration and attendance,
    II:102, IV:51–52
training on equipment use, IV:52,
    IV:61–62
training topics to be covered,
    II:102–3, III:117–18,
    IV:52–53, IV:63
visit with interviewee, IV:73–74
before-the-interview tasks of planners
    contacting potential interviewees,
        IV:48–49
    goals and, IV:47
    identifying and prioritizing poten-
        tial interviewees, IV:44–47
    matching interviewers with inter-
        viewees, IV:55–57
    timeline creation, IV:42–43
    training interviewers, IV:51–53,
        IV:61–63
before-the-interview tasks of project team
    background research materials
        development, IV:40–42
    overview of, 39–40, IV:17–18, IV:19
    standard recorded introduction to
        interviews development,
        IV:68
best practices
    inclusion of variety of community
        members, I:60–61
    laying groundwork for interviews,
        I:63
    OHA guidelines as benchmark,
        I:59–60, II:22–23
    oral history as process, I:60, II:23
    overview of, I:12–13, II:12–13,
        III:12–13, IV:12–13, V:16–17
    plan elements, I:61–62
    preservation of all materials, I:64
    sharing results, I:64–65
    technology choices, I:62

training of interviewers, I:63,
II:102–3
understanding ethical considerations, I:61
Best Practices (OHA), III:42
Best Practices for Oral History (OHA),
II:35
bias, issues of, I:53, IV:28–29
bibliography development for volunteers,
IV:40, IV:42
blogs, V:101
body language, IV:89, V:68
bookkeepers, III:54
books as possible outcomes, III:28,
V:120–23
Boyd, Douglas, III:87
Bradbury Science Museum (LANL),
V:128–30
Brown-Williams, Paula, V:126, V:127
Buckendorf, Madeline, II:46–47, III:110
budgets
developing several options, II:89
expense categories, II:59, II:88–89,
II:92, III:99–100
of fictitious projects, II:90, II:93
guidelines, II:88
income categories, II:91–92, II:96
prioritizing needs, II:93
project director responsibilities,
III:49, III:102–3
records management, III:49
sample, discussed, III:100–102
wrap-up steps, III:134
Buffalo Trace Oral History Project, I:52
Burnham, Angie, V:116–17
businesses, donations from local, III:98

C
California Roadside Heritage project,
V:126–28
card catalog management system, V:80
Carmel-by-the-Sea (California) Voices
Oral History Project. *See* volunteer fictitious project
cash gifts, II:96
catalogers (trained), III:54–55
cataloging
archives model, V:75–76

card catalog management, V:80
content management, V:81
database record keeping systems,
V:81–82
defining, II:100, V:77
elements of record, V:73
examples from fictitious projects,
II:101
Internet model, V:78
library management, V:81
library model, V:74–75
planning chart, V:85–86
processes to achieve successful,
V:78–79
protocol, I:75, I:84, V:86–87
reasons for, V:73
stand alone collection management,
V:80–81
terms, V:77
work sheet, V:32, V:88–89
Cataloging Planning Chart, V:85–86
Cataloging Protocol
about, V:86
sample, I:75, I:84, V:86–87
cataloging system, defining, V:77
Cataloging Work Sheet
described, V:32, V:88
processing and, V:32
sample, I:75, I:85, V:88–89
catalog records, defining, V:77
catalogs, defining, V:77
CDs, lifetime of, II:101
celebrations, examples of, III:136–37
challenges
finding expertise, I:36
identifying repository, I:37
insiders vs. outsiders, I:31–33
overview of, I:31
prevailing collective memories,
I:34–36
securing funding, I:38
working with volunteers, I:33–34
Chan, Roy, V:119–20
Chinatown Memory Map project,
V:118–20
city fictitious project
advisory committees and, II:34

budget, II:90, II:93
cataloging of, II:101
Cataloging Protocol, V:86–87
Cataloging Work Sheet, V:88–89
catalog management system, V:81
funding cycles and, II:51
Interviewee Biographical Profile
    Form, III:70, IV:66–67
Interviewee Recommendation
    Form, III:69
Interview Summary, III:73–74,
    IV:102–3
Interview Tracking Form, III:75–76
Legal Release Agreement, III:44–45,
    IV:36, V:147–48
Legal Release Agreement (Restric-
    tions), V:149–50
Letter of Agreement for Interviewer,
    III:60
Letter of Agreement for Repository,
    III:121
letter to potential interviewee, IV:49
management notes, III:34
overview of, II:23, II:24, III:20, III:21,
    III:34, V:80
Photograph and Memorabilia Re-
    ceipt, III:77–78, IV:99–100
Project Design Statement, III:35–37,
    V:139–42
team members, III:66–67
Team Member Time Sheet, III:62
work space, III:67
Civilian Conservation Corps (CCC),
    Minnesota project, I:28–29,
    III:136, V:121–23
class reunions, lessons from, I:23
closed questions, IV:83
closeness to issues as challenge, I:31–33
clothing for interviews, IV:77
COAT record keeping principles, V:40,
    V:54
collection management record keeping
    system, V:39
collective memory, I:22–23, I:34–36, IV:24
colleges, III:98
Colorado Fourmile Canyon Fire project,
    V:115–18
Colorado Voice Preserve, V:95

Columbia University, I:20
Commission of Deaf, DeafBlind, and
    Hard of Hearing Minnesotans
    Oral-Visual Project, II:21, II:22,
    II:23
committees, II:34, III:18
community
    access to results, I:64–65, V:100–101
    advisory committees/boards and,
        II:34
    building through oral history,
        V:109–10
    defining, I:10, I:28, II:10, II:22, III:10,
        III:20, IV:10, V:14
    developing focus with, II:49
    documenting contributions from
        supporters, III:99
    effect on, V:133–34
    forums, V:101
    funding sources in, II:93–94
    identifying resources in, II:34
    inclusion of all appropriate mem-
        bers, I:12, I:60–61, II:12,
        III:12, IV:12, IV:29, V:16
    involvement in public events, V:109
    management of supporters, III:48,
        III:63
    of memory, I:29
    public relations and, III:134
    representing project to, III:48
    role during management phase,
        III:24, III:25
    role in planning, II:32–34, II:105
    sharing interviews with, III:108–9
    sharing success with, I:13, II:13,
        III:13, IV:13, V:17
    as source of currently available
        information, IV:42
community oral history, defining, II:22,
    III:20
community oral history projects
    defining, I:10, II:10, II:23, III:10,
        III:20, IV:10, V:14
    differences with academic projects,
        I:10, II:10, III:10, IV:10, V:14
    overview of best practices, I:12–13,
        II:12–13, III:12–13, IV:12–
        13, V:16–17

computers and accessories
    choosing, II:83–84, II:122–23
    standards, II:123–24
confidentiality issues
    access and, III:65, III:79
    legal release and, V:28
    transparency and, III:108
consistency
    commitment to project duration by
        team members, III:48, III:55
    importance of, III:49
    in record keeping, V:40
consultants
    as planning director, II:32
    roles of, III:28, III:55
    typical number of interviews by,
        III:111
content management system (CMS), V:81
contextual materials, packaging, V:27,
    V:53
contextual notes
    benefits of, IV:30
    example of, IV:105–6
    information to include, IV:103,
        IV:105
    post-interview preparation of,
        IV:107
controlled vocabulary, V:83–84, V:156n.10
controversy, dealing with, IV:84–85
conversational trap, IV:83
copyright
    laws, II:36–37
    legal definition of, II:36
    legal release agreements and, I:55,
        II:39, III:42, IV:33, IV:34
    quotations from interviews and,
        V:109
    repository and, V:37, V:155n.2
    transfer of, II:37, II:127n.8
Copyright Act (1976), II:36–37
curators, V:31
Cushman Motor Works Project in Lin-
    coln, Nebraska, I:46, II:21, II:22,
    III:27–28, IV:43

D
database record keeping systems, V:39,
    V:81–82

data files
    audio compared to video, II:82
    preservation kit, III:87
    storage, II:79, II:81, II:92, III:84–85
D-Day oral history, I:20
Deck, Linda, V:130
deeds of gift, II:38
    See also Legal Release Agreement;
        Legal Release Agreement
        (Restrictions)
Democracy in America (de Tocqueville),
    I:33
Densho Digital Archive website, II:66
Densho: Japanese American Legacy
    Project, II:66
derivative works, creation and copyright
    of, II:37
design
    goals and, II:46
    planning and, II:26
    statement of decisions, II:44–46
de Tocqueville, Alexis, I:33
devil's advocate, playing, IV:85
digital files/recordings
    fragility of, V:96, V:97
    maps, V:119–20
    media-free, V:96
    media migration issues, II:101
    metadata, V:98
    multiple copies in different formats/
        media, V:100
digital libraries, II:65
Digital Millennium Act (1998), II:36–37
digital repositories, II:66, II:101, V:22,
    V:27, V:94–95
display and copyright, II:37
distribution and copyright, II:37
documentation
    on all physical media, V:41–42
    of assessment results post interview,
        V:24
    of changes, III:113
    of contributions from community
        supporters, III:99
    of disposition of master files, V:41,
        V:105
    of dollar value of volunteers, III:67
    for interviews, V:46–49

management of forms, III:68
multiple copies of, V:99–100
of people involved in project,
V:42–45
production of manual of project,
V:105–7
record keeping rules in, V:40
See also files; record keeping; sample
forms
donations
overview of, II:91, II:96
on sample budget, III:100–101
tips for acquiring, III:98
value of, III:97
donor forms. See Legal Release Agreement; Legal Release Agreement
(Restrictions)
driving tour outcome example, V:125–28
Dublin Core, V:77, V:82, V:87
Dudding, Michael, V:69, V:155n.9
duration
copyright and, V:155n.2
determining project, II:51–52
extending project, V:25
maximum effective, for interviews,
IV:92–93
of processing stage, V:23
of training workshops, II:102, IV:51
See also time
dynamic websites, V:102

E
EAD, V:77, V:82
Eastern Sierra Institute for Collaborative
Education (ESICE), V:126–28
email as substitute for recorded interview,
I:42
email contact of potential interviewees,
IV:48
emotions of interviewees, I:53, IV:30–31
envelope, after-the-interview, III:125,
III:126
equipment
computers and accessories, II:83–84,
II:122–24
disposition at project end, V:104
evolving formats and preservation,
I:48

growth of oral history projects and,
I:62
obtaining, I:38
See also audio recording equipment;
recording equipment; video
recording equipment
ethical considerations
bias issues, I:53, IV:28–29
equipment selection, I:54
establishing historical context, I:56–57
exploiting vulnerable people,
I:53–54
funding, I:55–56
importance of understanding, I:61
for interview management,
III:108–10
Legal Release Agreements, I:55
OHA guidelines, III:42
online access, II:65
overview of, I:12, I:52–54, II:12,
III:12, IV:12, V:16
of post-interview tasks, IV:32
repository choice, I:54–55
transparency of purpose, I:52
ethical considerations for interviewers
before-the-interview, IV:28–30
during-the-interview, IV:30–32
post-interview, IV:32
exhibits
outcome example, V:128–30
processing and, V:36
expenses
categories of, II:59, II:88–89, II:92,
III:99–100
in sample budget, III:100–101
expertise, challenge of finding, I:36–37
external hard drives, choosing, II:83–84
external microphones, advantages of,
III:84, III:86

F
Facebook, IV:45, V:101
face-to-face issues, I:42
facial expressions, V:68
fair use, described, III:109
family history
Bibles, I:17
interviews, I:27

as storytelling, I:25–26
Federal Writer's Project, I:20
fictitious oral history project examples.
          See city fictitious project; historical
          society fictitious project; volunteer
          fictitious project
fields (database), V:81–82
files
          audio compared to video data files,
                    II:82
          confidentiality and access, III:79
          data file preservation kit, III:87
          importance of, III:78, III:80
          storage of data files, II:75, II:76,
                    II:79, II:81, II:92, II:99,
                    III:84–85
          suggested materials for interviewee,
                    III:79
          suggested materials for project,
                    III:78–79
          See also digital files/recordings
film outcome example, V:115–18
finding aids, V:75–76, V:77
fiscal sponsors, II:92, II:96
fiscal sponsors/agents, described, III:94
focus. *See* project (historical focus)
Fogerty, James E., II:97
folklorists compared to oral historians,
          I:27
follow-up interviews, IV:81, IV:93, IV:94
follow-up questions, IV:21, IV:42, IV:64,
          IV:69–70, IV:84
forms
          for funds management, III:97
          as management tools, III:68
          for recording equipment kit, III:86
          reviewing and managing, III:49
          See also sample forms
Fourmile Canyon Fire, Colorado project,
          V:115–18
Frankfort, Kentucky, Buffalo Trace Distill-
          ery project, I:52
Freedom of Information Act requests,
          III:110
Frisch, Michael, V:68
Froh, Geoff, V:97
From Secrecy to Accessibility: The Rocky

Flats Cold War Museum Plant
          Oral Histories in boulder Colo-
          rado, III:129
funders
          ethics and agendas of, IV:28, IV:29
          role during management phase,
                    III:24, III:25
funding
          categories, II:91–92, II:96
          challenge of securing, I:38
          community sources, II:93–94
          defining, III:92
          documentation requirements, III:67,
                    III:97
          donations, III:97–98
          ethical considerations, I:55–56
          examples of sources, II:94, III:92–93
          following OHA guidelines as crite-
                    ria for, I:60
          goals of sources of, II:95
          national sources, II:95
          need for additional, V:25
          project cycles/duration, II:51–52
          solicited, II:96
          state sources, II:94
          See also grants

G

genealogists, oral historians compared
          to, I:27
General Principles for Oral History (OHA),
          II:35, III:42
goals
          of all oral history, V:36
          assessment of accomplishments,
                    V:24
          design and, II:46
          examples of primary, II:47
          familiarization of interviewer with,
                    IV:60
          focus on, during interviews, IV:55,
                    IV:56, IV:61
          funders and, II:95
          grant requirements and, III:97
          historical focus and, III:106
          importance of realistic, IV:47
          refining during management, III:28
          short-term and processing, V:36

gossip, avoiding, IV:31, IV:32, IV:65
grants
    fiscal sponsors and, II:92, II:96
    overview of, II:91
    requirements, III:67, III:94, III:97
    on sample budget, III:100–101
    sources of, II:94, III:93
    timeframes defined by, V:25
    workshops for writing, II:96
    writing, III:27, III:94–97
Greene, Mark A., V:36, V:155n.1
Greenwich, Connecticut Library Oral
    History Project, III:63, III:113
griots, I:17
group interviews, III:115–16, IV:47
Guide to Oral History and the Law, A
    (Neuenschwander), II:36, II:37,
    III:109, IV:27, IV:33

H
Halls High View Park Archive Project in
    Arlington, VA, V:110
Hard Work and a Good Deal: the Civilian
    Conservation Corps in Minnesota
    (Sommer), V:121–23
Hawley, Elizabeth Haven, III:91
high school yearbooks, as sources of
    interviewee-specific information,
    IV:64
historians, role of, I:18
historical context
    discovering, I:19
    importance of, III:107, IV:29–30
    for interviews, I:17
historical focus. See project (historical)
    focus
historical record
    defining, V:99
    elements of, I:18
    incompleteness of, I:19
    objectivity of, I:19–20
historical societies
    advantages of ties to, III:21
    aid in writing grants, III:27
    as resources, I:37, IV:42, IV:64
historical society fictitious project
    advantages of ties to historical
        society, III:21

    advisory committees and, II:34
    budget, II:93, III:103
    cataloging of, II:101
    catalog management system,
        V:80–81
    described, V:80
    focus, II:49
    internal milestones, II:51
    management notes, III:38
    overview of, II:23, II:24, III:20, III:21,
        III:38, V:80
    Project Design Statement, III:39–41,
        V:143–46
    team members, III:67
    work space, III:67
history from the ground up, I:21
History of California (Bancroft), I:20
Hoffman, Alice, IV:83
H-Oralhist listserv, I:36, III:120
Huang, Anne, II:17–18, V:118
humanities councils, as resource, I:37,
    III:93

I
ideas, transition to planning from,
    II:29–30
income
    generated by project, III:110
    on sample budget, III:100–102
    See also funding; grants
index to interviews, III:126
India Association of Minnesota Oral His-
    tory Project, II:43
information units, V:77, V:81
in-kind support, I:38, II:91, III:67
In Our Own Words project, III:137
insider/outsider issues, I:31–33, III:114–
    15, IV:55
Institute of Museum and Library Services
    (IMLS), III:93
interactive websites, V:102
Internet
    abstracts of interviews available on,
        III:127
    cataloging model, V:78
    categories of oral histories on, V:27
    emails to contact potential inter-
        viewees, IV:48

processing for, V:53
proper use of, III:122
as repository, II:66
as research tool, IV:41–42
restrictions on publication on, IV:35
as source of interview questions,
    IV:72
YouTube, V:97
See also digital repositories; websites
Internet, access on
advantages of, I:48
ethical and legal considerations,
    II:65
ideas for, V:101–2
levels of, II:65–66
media migration and, II:101
website budgeting, II:59
interns, III:55
interpretative monologue, V:123
interpretative online sites, V:27, V:118–20
Interviewee Biographical Profile form
about, II:67, III:70, V:44
management notes, III:70
sample, I:74, I:79, II:69, III:70–72,
    IV:66–67, V:44–45
as source of background informa-
    tion, IV:65
Interviewee Recommendation Form
about, II:67, III:68
management notes, III:68
sample, I:74, I:78, II:68, III:69
interviewees
accents of, as challenge, I:48
anonymity of, I:27, III:115
as authors of recorded interviews,
    II:35–36, II:37
benefits of transcripts to, V:56
Biographical Profile, V:44–45
body language and, IV:89
changes in list of, III:113–14
clothing for video, IV:77
contacting potential, IV:48–49
copyright and, IV:33, IV:34
criteria for, III:112–13, IV:44, IV:46
dealing with nervous, IV:80
definition of, II:20
effect on, V:133–34
emotions of, I:53, IV:30–31

ethics and legal release agreements,
    I:55
honoring, V:109
identifying and prioritizing poten-
    tial, II:55–56, IV:44–47
importance of inclusivity, III:112,
    IV:29
information about other topics
    from, IV:61
Master Contact List of, V:42–43
matching with interviewers, III:114,
    IV:55–57
memories of jogging, IV:24–25,
    IV:91–92
memories of untrue, IV:25, IV:82
photos/memoribilia of, IV:91, IV:92,
    IV:98, IV:107
planning for multi-sided historical
    focus, II:49
potential for exploitation of, I:53–54
prominent people as, IV:44
recruiting, III:114, IV:45
rehearsed stories from, IV:88
remuneration for, III:110
research specific to each, IV:64–65
respecting requests of, V:27–29
review of transcript by, I:48, V:52,
    V:63
suggested materials for files, III:79
tone of language, IV:90
unfamiliar use of vocabulary by,
    IV:88
visit with, before interview, IV:73–74
See also Legal Release Agreement;
    Legal Release Agreement
    (Restrictions)
interviewers
ability to elicit forgotten memories,
    IV:24–25, IV:91–92
as authors of recorded interviews,
    II:35–36, II:37
background materials and, IV:40–
    42, IV:91
before-the-interview ethical consid-
    erations, IV:28–30
body language and, IV:89
characteristics of effective, III:52–53,
    IV:50–52, IV:80

clothing for video, IV:77
copyright and, IV:33
dealing with controversy, IV:84–85
dealing with rehearsed stories, IV:88
dealing with talkative interviewees,
    IV:100–101
dealing with untrue memories,
    IV:25, IV:82
description of responsibilities,
    III:57–58
during-the-interview tasks, IV:20
ethics and legal release agreements,
    I:55
follow-up questions from, IV:21,
    IV:42, IV:64, IV:69–70, IV:84
importance of tone, IV:72, IV:83
interruptions by, IV:86–87
interviewing each other as training,
    IV:51
keeping track of interview time,
    IV:92–93
Letter of Agreement for Interviewer,
    II:72, III:60
Master Contact List of, V:42–43
matching with interviewees, III:114,
    IV:55–57
number of interviews per, II:52
one question at a time rule, IV:86
as partner of interviewee, IV:31
preparation time for interviews,
    III:111
professionalism, IV:74
recording equipment training work-
    shops, III:88–90
responsibilities, III:52
steps before conducting interviews,
    I:69–70
training, importance of, I:13, I:63,
    II:13, III:13, III:50, IV:13,
    IV:51, V:17
training duration and attendance,
    II:102, IV:51–52
training on equipment use, IV:52,
    IV:61–62
training topics to be covered,
    III:117–18, IV:52–53, IV:63
as transcribers, III:53, V:52, V:59
transcribing and, IV:106, IV:107

use of silence, IV:86
using mentors, III:118
using research notes during inter-
    views, IV:90
See also before-the-interview tasks
    of interviewers; post-inter-
    view tasks of interviewers;
    questions, asking
Interview ID, V:41, V:50
interviewing kits, items to include, IV:75
interview log/index, described, III:126
interview processing, steps, I:71
interviews
    abstracts of, III:127
    academic projects, I:20
    authors of, II:35–36, II:37
    as basis for secondary sources, V:114
    as beginning of oral history, V:91
    Cataloging Work Sheet for each,
        V:88–89
    community and content, III:24, III:25
    compared to other primary sources,
        IV:81
    containing performances, III:110
    data format for recording, IV:62
    defining, IV:21, IV:22–23
    directions to, IV:75
    eating/drinking during, IV:80
    elements of, I:26
    email, I:42
    ending gracefully, IV:93–94
    ethical considerations before,
        IV:28–30
    ethical considerations during,
        IV:30–32
    ethical/legal management consider-
        ations, III:108–10
    follow-up questions during, IV:21,
        IV:42, IV:64, IV:69–70, IV:84
    funders and content, III:24, III:25
    goals and, IV:47, IV:55, IV:56
    historical focus and content of, II:50
    importance of context, I:17, I:52,
        III:107, IV:29–30
    importance of groundwork, I:13,
        I:63, II:13, III:13, IV:13, V:17
    interviewees desire to withdraw all
        or part of, V:28

introducing follow-up, IV:81
introduction to, IV:68, IV:80–81
legal disclosure of, IV:31–32
Letter of Agreement for Repository
    processing requirements for,
    III:111, III:125
lost, III:123
making multiple copies of, V:50,
    V:51, V:52, V:53, V:62, V:98,
    V:99–100
management support of, III:24–25
mission statement and, IV:65
multi-person, III:115–16, IV:47
number of, II:52, III:111–12
outline development for, IV:67–72
planning step-by-step, I:69–70
preservation of, I:13, I:64, II:13,
    III:13, III:127, IV:13, V:17
as primary sources, I:18–19, IV:23,
    V:113, V:114
props for, IV:76
recorded hours for each, III:111
record keeping, V:46–49
reviewing specific subjects/themes
    to cover, III:106–7
routine nature of many, IV:51
scheduling, III:116, IV:73–74, V:25
second, for recording, IV:78
set-up at location, IV:76–78
sharing with community, III:108–9
as snapshot of history, V:92
space needs for, II:75–76, III:65
steps after, I:70–71
telephone, I:42
unique ID for each, V:41
use of quotations from, III:110,
    V:109
using outline, IV:81
using research notes during, IV:90
wrap-up steps, III:133–34
See also entries beginning with
    before-the-interview tasks;
    entries beginning with
    post-interview tasks; entries
    beginning with *transcri;*
    processing
Interview Summary
    about, II:67, II:99, III:72, V:32

as abstract, V:69
example of, IV:104
importance of, IV:101, IV:103
processing and, V:32
sample, I:74, I:80, II:70, III:73–74,
    IV:102–3, V:46–47
used for recording abstract, III:126
Interview Tracking Form
    about, II:70–71, III:74
    management notes, III:75
    sample, I:74, I:82, II:71, III:75–76,
        V:48–49
    use of multiple, V:155n.5
iPhones as recording equipment, III:84
It Takes a Village to Make a City: Duluth
    (MN) Residents Speak Out Oral
    History Project. *See* historical
    society fictitious project

J
jargon
    checking, IV:95
    familiarity with unique project,
        IV:64
    unfamiliar use of, by interviewee,
        IV:88
Jazz Atlanta Oral History Project. *See* city
    fictitious project
Jefferson, Thomas, V:99
journalists, oral historians compared to,
    I:27–28

K
Kaufman, Moisés, V:123
Kennedy, Steve, I:29–30
keyword tags, V:69
Kohn, Ammi, V:124–25

L
Lama Foundation Library of Oral History
    and Memory project, V:124–25
language
    controlled vocabulary, V:83–84,
        V:156n.10
    facial and body, IV:89, V:68
    jargon, IV:64, IV:88, IV:95
    tone of, IV:72
    use of neutral, V:40

Laramie Project, V:123
leading questions, IV:83
Lee, Spike, V:115
legal considerations
    disclosure of information in inter-
        views, IV:31–32
    ethics and Legal Release Agreements,
        I:55
    for interview management,
        III:108–10
    need for legal expert on team, III:55
    online access, II:65
    overview of, I:12, II:12, III:12, IV:12,
        V:16
    planning and, II:38
    standards, II:26–27
    terms, III:109
    See also copyright; Legal Release
        Agreement; Legal Release
        Agreement (Restrictions)
Legal Release Agreement
    about, II:35–36, II:37, II:38, II:67
    appropriateness to project, IV:35
    city fictitious project, III:44, IV:36,
        V:147–48
    completing, IV:98, IV:107
    components of, II:38–39
    copyright and, II:39, IV:33
    described, V:31
    developing, II:39, IV:33–34
    management notes, III:42–43
    processing and, V:26, V:31
    responsibilities of project director,
        III:108
    sample, I:75, I:86, II:40, III:44, IV:36,
        V:147–48
Legal Release Agreement (Restrictions)
    about, II:67, III:43, IV:35
    city fictitious project, III:45,
        V:149–50
    developing, II:39
    legal strength of, III:110
    management notes, III:46
    managing, V:28
    sample, I:75–76, I:87, II:41, III:45,
        IV:37, V:149–50
Letter of Agreement for Interviewer

about, II:72, III:59, III:64
    management notes, III:59
    sample, I:76, I:89, II:72, III:60, IV:54
    signing of, IV:53
Letter of Agreement for Repository
    about, II:63–64, II:70–71, II:72,
        III:120
    described, V:31
    processing and, V:31
    processing requirements of, III:111,
        III:125
    sample, I:76, I:88, II:63, III:121, V:30
Letter of Agreement for Transcriber
    about, II:72, III:59, III:64
    management notes, III:59
    sample, I:76, I:90, II:73, III:61, V:65
Letters of Understanding. See specific Let-
    ters of Agreement
letters to potential interviewees, IV:48–49
libel, III:109
libraries
    as office/storage space, II:76
    as partners, I:46, III:98
    as repositories, II:102, III:124, V:93,
        V:94
    as source of cataloging information,
        III:54
library management system, V:81
library model of cataloging, V:74–75
Library Oral History Project in Green-
    wich, Connecticut, III:63, III:113
Lincoln, Nebraska, Cushman Motor
    Works project, I:46, II:21, II:22,
        III:27–28, IV:43
listening, importance of, IV:50–51
listserv, H-Oralhist, III:120
loans, sources of non-monetary, III:98
local sources of information, IV:42
LOCKSS (Lots of Copies Keeps Stuff
    Safe) principle, III:125, V:99–100,
        V:156n.16
Los Alamos National Laboratory (LANL),
    V:128–30
Louie B. Nunn Center for Oral History at
    University of Kentucky, I:52
M
machine dependent, defining, V:99
management

guiding structure, III:29
overview of steps, I:68–69, III:22–25
principles, III:24–25
survey respondents, III:148–49
survey sample, III:139–47
management notes
    city fictitious project, III:34
    historical society fictitious project,
        III:38
    for Interviewee Biographical Profile
        Form, III:70
    for Interviewee Recommendation
        Form, III:68
    for Interview Summary, III:72–73
    for Interview Tracking Form, III:75
    for Legal Release Agreement,
        III:42–43
    for Legal Release Agreement (Re-
        strictions), III:46
    for Letters of Agreement, III:59
    for Photograph and Memorabilia
        Receipt, III:76–77
    volunteer fictitious project, III:30
MARC, V:74, V:75, V:77, V:82, V:87
Maria Rogers Oral History Program,
    I:56–57, II:64, II:66, III:129
Master Contact List, V:42–43
master documents, V:40–41, V:105,
    V:155n.3
McLeod, Susan, III:105
media, described, III:86
media-free digital files, V:96
media management, planning, II:99
Meissner, Dennis, V:36, V:155n.1
Melnick, aj, V:129
memorabilia, II:74, IV:91, IV:98–100, IV:107
    See also Photograph and Memora-
        bilia Receipt
memory map outcome example,
    V:118–20
memory/memories
    art as aid, I:17
    CCC as community of, I:29
    characteristics of, IV:24–25
    collective, I:22–23, I:34–36, IV:24
    dealing with untrue, IV:25, IV:82
    eliciting forgotten, IV:24–25,
        IV:91–92

of events, I:22, IV:24
failing, of interviewees, IV:91
hidden, I:35–36
malleability of, I:21–22, I:23
oral history and, I:21–23
reinterpretation of, IV:25
mentor interviewers, III:118
Mercier, Laurie, II:46–47, III:110
metadata, II:100, V:82, V:98
    defining, III:125, III:126, V:77, V:99
metadata schemes, defining, V:77
Michigan Advent House Ministries proj-
    ect, III:135–36
microphones
    advantages of external, III:84, III:86
    budgeting for, II:92
    choosing, II:82–83
    set-up at interview location of,
        IV:76, IV:80
    standards, II:121
Minnesota Civilian Conservation Corps
    Documentation Project, I:28–29,
    III:136, V:121–23
Minnesota Digital Library website, II:66
Minnesota Historical and Cultural Grants
    Manual oral history guidelines,
    III:94–96
Minnesota Historical Society
    India Association project, II:43
    Smith Club project, II:97–98
    website, II:66
Minnesota India Association project, II:43
Minnesota Smith Club project, II:97–98
mission statement
    developing, II:53–54
    examples of, II:54
    grant requirements and, III:97
    as guide for choosing interviewees,
        III:113
    historical focus and, III:106
    interviews and, IV:65
    on Legal Release Agreement, II:40
    maintaining focus on, III:49
    overview of, III:28
    Project Design Statement and, II:44
    purpose of, I:52
    reviewing, III:107
    team recruitment and, III:55

mistakes, repetition of, V:40
monetary sources. *See* funding
Montana Historical Society website, II:66
Moulton, George, V:129 (photo), V:130
multi-person interviews, III:115–16, IV:47
multi-sided historical focus, II:49

N
name of project
    examples of, II:53
    importance of, II:19, II:53
    overview of, III:28
name tags, V:69
narrative, prevailing
    establishment of prevailing, I:34–35
    responsibility to go beyond, I:22–23
narrators. *See* interviewees
National Association of Interpretation,
    V:127–28
National Endowment for the Arts (NEA),
    III:93
National Endowment for the Humanities
    (NEH), III:93
national funding sources, II:95
National Historical Publications and
    Records Commission (NHPRC),
    III:93
national sources of grants, III:93
Negro Spiritual Heritage Keepers Project,
    The, III:137
Nelson, Cyns, I:30, V:95
Nelson, Ed, V:121
Neuenschwander, John, II:36, II:37, II:38,
    III:109, IV:27, IV:33
neutral questions, IV:83
New Mexico Lama Foundation project,
    V:124–25
newspapers, IV:42
noise, background, II:75
non-profit status issue, III:94
non-recurring expenses, II:88, II:92, III:99
Northeast Minnesota Historical Center
    website, II:66

O
Oakland Asian Cultural Center, II:17–18,
    II:66
Oakland Chinatown Oral History Project,
    II:66

Oakland (California) Chinatown Oral
    History Project (OCOHP),
    V:118–20
objectivity, I:19–20, V:40
office staff, III:54
Ogden, Catherine H., III:63, III:113
one-time expenses, described, II:88, II:92,
    III:99
online access
    ethical and legal considerations,
        II:65
    levels of, II:65–66
    media migration and, II:101
    website budgeting, II:59
    See also Internet, access on
online chats, as oral history interview, I:42
online public access catalogs (OPACs),
    V:78
open-ended questions, IV:83
open file format, V:99
operating costs, II:89, II:92
oral historians
    folklorists compared to, I:27
    genealogists compared to, I:27
    journalists compared to, I:27–28
    responsibility to go beyond public
        stories, I:22–23
    sociologists compared to, I:26–27
oral history
    accessibility of, I:23
    defining, I:11, I:26, I:27, II:11, II:20,
        III:11, IV:11, V:15
    effect of, V:133–34
    elements, III:20
    ethical and legal considerations,
        V:16, V:109
    evolution of, I:20–21
    finding out whys and hows, IV:45
    goal of, V:36
    going beyond already known, IV:45
    importance of, V:92–93
    interviews as beginning of, V:91
    as living window into past, I:22
    memory and, I:21–32
    as primary source material, IV:21,
        IV:23, IV:81–82
    as process, I:12, II:12, III:12, IV:12,
        V:16

storytelling compared to, I:17
uses of, III:132
Oral History and the Law (Neuen-
    schwander), II:36
Oral History Association (OHA)
    availability of guidelines, III:42
    definition of community, I:28
    guidelines titles and website, II:35
    importance of guidelines, I:12, I:36,
        I:59–60, II:12, II:22–23,
        III:12, IV:12, V:16
    website, III:42, III:120
Oral History in the Digital Age (OHDA)
    website, III:83
oral history programs, defining, III:22
oral history project decisions
    record-keeping, I:42–43
    repository determination, I:46–47
    technology, I:39–42
oral history project examples
    Advent House Ministries in Michi-
        gan, III:135–36
    Buffalo Trace Distillery in Frankfort,
        Kentucky, I:52
    CCC in Minnesota, I:28–29, III:136,
        V:121–23
    Commission of Deaf, DeafBlind,
        and Hard of Hearing Min-
        nesotans, II:21, II:22, II:23
    Cushman Motor Works in Ne-
        braska, I:46, II:21, II:22,
        III:27–28, IV:43
    fictitious (*See* city fictitious project;
        historical society fictitious
        project; volunteer fictitious
        project)
    Fourmile Canyon Fire, Colorado
        project, V:115–18
    Greenwich Library in Connecticut,
        III:63, III:113
    India Association of Minnesota, II:43
    Lama Foundation Library of Oral
        History and Memory proj-
        ect, V:124–25
    Los Alamos National Laboratory
        "They Changed the World"
        exhibit, V:128–30
    Oakland Asian Cultural Center,

        II:17–18
    Oakland (California) Chinatown
        Oral History Project (OC-
        OHP), V:118–20
    In Our Own Words, III:137
    Roadside Heritage, California,
        V:126–28
    Rocky Flats Cold War Museum,
        I:56–57, III:129
    Smith Club of Minnesota, II:97–98
    2008 election in Arapahoe County,
        Colorado, I:29–30
    Women in Journalism Oral History
        Project, IV:46
Oral History Project in Greenwich, Con-
    necticut, III:63, III:113
oral history projects
    defining, III:22
    ethics and agendas of partners,
        IV:28, IV:29
    as genesis of future oral history
        projects, IV:61
    purposes of, I:45–46
oral tradition, universality of, I:17
oral-visual history projects, II:21, II:22, II:23
orientation meetings, III:62–63
outcomes, I:49, V:131
    access and, I:45
    books, III:28, III:136, V:120–22
    exhibit, V:128–30
    film, V:115–18
    importance of transcripts to, III:129
    interactive website, V:118–20
    as part of project management,
        III:24, III:25
    public events, V:109
    publicity about, V:105
    school curriculum, V:122–23
    as secondary sources, V:113, V:114
    spin-off projects from, V:122–23
    theater, V:123–25
    transcripts for repurposing, V:57
    walking/driving tour, V:125–28
outreach plans, III:50, V:105
outsider/insider issues, I:31–33, III:114–
    15, IV:55
overhead costs, described, II:89, II:92,
    III:99–100

P

packaging, V:27, V:53–54

PACKED (film), V:116–18

paper as preservation format, V:57, V:98, V:156n.15

paper record keeping system, V:39

paperwork. *See* documentation; record keeping

parameters, importance of articulating, I:52

partnerships, obtaining donations from, III:98

People Who Made It Work: A Centennial History of Cushman Motor Works, The, III:28

performance evaluations, as grant requirement, III:97

performances in interviews, III:110

per-interview costs, described, II:89, II:92, III:100

permanent contact, V:104

personnel

Master Contact List of, V:42–43

planning team members, II:32

See also volunteers; *specific roles such as interviewers*

Photograph and Memorabilia Receipt

about, II:74, III:76, IIII:98

management notes, III:76–77

sample, I:74, I:81, II:74, III:77–78, IV:99–100

photographs

as donations, IV:91

loan of, IV:98, IV:107

using in interviews, IV:24, IV:92

planning

assessment of and adjustments to, V:23–24

decisions required, II:31

decision tracking, II:44–46

design statement, II:44–46

director, II:32

goals and, II:46

guiding questions for, II:30–31

importance of, II:23, II:24–26, II:27–28

overview of, I:13, I:61–62, II:13, II:26–27, II:51, II:105, III:13, V:17

prioritizing needs, II:93

project team members, II:57–58

resources available, II:35

step-by-step overview of, I:67–68

survey questions, II:107–12

survey respondents, II:113–14

time spent, III:18

transition from idea to, II:29–30

work space needs, II:75–76

See also specific topics

planning team members, II:32, III:24

Pogue, Forrest, I:20

post-interview tasks

assessment of project status, V:23–25

ethical considerations, IV:32

immediate, III:124, V:49–50

Interview Summary, V:46–47

Letter of Agreement for Repository processing requirements, III:111, III:125

LOCKSS principle, III:125

media management, II:99

notes and forms, V:50

overview of, I:70–71, II:98

packaging, V:27

project director responsibilities, III:50

record keeping, II:99

repository and, II:100–101, V:26

See also cataloging; entries beginning with *transcri;* preservation; processing

post-interview tasks of interviewers

audit-checking, V:63

collection of all items for repository, IV:108

equipment handling, IV:100

immediate, IV:97–98

Interview Summary, IV:101–3, V:46–47

Legal Release Agreement, IV:33, IV:98

making copies of interview, IV:101

overview of, IV:20, IV:53

recording handling, III:33, V:50

record keeping, IV:107–8, V:49–50

preservation

access and, V:93
audio compared to video files, II:82
of audio files of interviews, I:48
defining, III:124, V:91, V:99
evolving technology and, I:48
formats, V:57, V:95–98, V:156n.15
importance of multiple copies,
　　III:125
of interviews, I:13, II:13, III:13,
　　IV:13, V:17
long-term, III:126–28
as purpose of project, I:45–46
repository identification and, I:47
steps, III:125, III:133–34
terms used, III:126
of verbatim transcripts, I:48–49
video issues, I:41, I:42
See also entries beginning with
　　transcri; repositories
preservation master (copy), V:50
primary sources
examples of, I:18–19
firsthand knowledge of interview-
　　ees, IV:44
objectivity of, I:19–20
oral history as, IV:21, IV:23,
　　IV:81–82
purposes behind, I:19
role in oral history, I:26
secondary sources vs., V:113, V:114
private funding sources, II:93–94
pro bono expertise from professionals,
　　III:98
process, defining, II:23
processing
access and, II:101
allocation of responsibilities for, V:32
assignment of Interview ID, V:50
defining, V:22, V:36
examples from fictitious projects,
　　II:101
forms for, V:31–32
importance of, II:99, III:111, V:21,
　　V:22
individuals involved in, V:23
Letter of Agreement for Repository
　　requirements, III:111, III:125
Master Contact List of personnel,

V:42–43
media-free, V:96
options, II:98–100
overview of, II:98
packaging interviews, V:27, V:53
planning for, II:99–100, V:36–38
Project Design Statement and, V:31
project usage and, V:36
reviewing, V:104
skills required, V:33
time requirements, III:111–12, V:23,
　　V:26
training for, V:26
user-centered approach, V:155n.1
See also cataloging; entries begin-
　　ning with transcri
processing steps
acknowledgements, V:54, V:105,
　　V:108
media management, V:50–51
overview of, V:32–33
repository, V:52–54
transcription, V:52
See also record keeping
processing team members
interviewer tasks, V:49–50, V:52
Master Contact List of personnel,
　　V:42–43
project director tasks, V:49–54
skills needed, V:26
transcriber tasks, V:52
processors (trained), III:54–55
Project Design Statement
about, II:44, II:46, II:67
city fictitious project, III:35–37,
　　V:139–42
described, V:31
historical society fictitious project,
　　III:39–41, V:143–46
as management guide, III:29
processing and, V:31
as reflection of reality, V:24
sample, I:74, I:77, II:45
updating, III:107, III:113
volunteer fictitious project, III:31–
　　33, V:135–38
project director
budget responsibilities, III:102–3

control of access to computer applications, V:39–40
determination of paid and volunteer positions, III:66
documentation of assessment meeting, V:24
equipment management responsibilities, III:82, III:84, III:87–88
external responsibilities, III:48
finding repository as priority, III:120
indexing decisions, IV:107
internal responsibilities, III:49–50, III:53, III:107
Legal Release Agreement responsibilities, III:108
maintaining interest of volunteers, IV:32
preservation responsibilities, III:126, III:128
processing tasks, V:49–54
public relations responsibilities, III:50, V:105
requirements, III:48
team management tips, III:58
transcribing decisions, IV:106, V:59
project (historical) focus
articulation of, I:52
context planning and, II:50
dealing with new topics, III:107
described, II:46–47, III:29
developing, II:47–49
documenting changes, III:113
importance of, III:106
interview content planning and, II:50
interviewee planning and, II:49
maintaining, III:49, III:113
reviewing, III:106–7
timeline for, IV:42–43
project forms. See forms; sample forms
project interviewee list, II:55–56
project manual, producing, V:105–7
project scope
elements of, III:29
reviewing, III:107
project team
assembling of interviewing kits by, IV:75
development of background re-

search materials by, IV:40–42
development of standard recorded introduction to interviews by, IV:68
overview of, II:57–58, IV:19
transcribing decisions by, IV:106
project team members
bookkeepers/accountants, III:54
city fictitious project, III:66–67
collaboration among, III:52
consultants, III:28, III:55, III:111
familiarity with already available information, IV:40
historical society fictitious project, III:67
management tips, III:58
office staff, III:54
ongoing meetings, III:56
optional, III:55
orientation meetings, III:62–63
overview of, II:57–58, III:51–52
processors/catalogers (trained), III:54–55
project director, III:48–50
of projects with organizational affiliations, III:67
recorder maintenance technicians, III:54
recording technicians, III:53–54
recruiting, III:55–58
reviewing updated Project Design Statement with, III:107
supervising, III:49
time sheets, III:62
volunteer fictitious project, III:66
See also specific roles such as interviewers
project wrap-up steps, III:133–34
public advocacy, as overt purpose of project, IV:28
publication, processing and, V:36
public events, holding, V:109
public face, project director as, III:48
public libraries, as partners, I:46
public performance and copyright, II:37
public relations
celebrations as, III:136–37
community and, III:134

example of exhibit invitation,
III:135–36
as responsibility of project director,
III:50, V:105
public stories
establishment of, I:34–35
responsibility of oral historians to
go beyond, I:22–23

Q

questionable situations, dealing with,
III:109–10
questionnaires, with predetermined
choices, I:26–27
questions, asking
about undisputed factual information, IV:91
controversial, IV:85
follow-up, IV:21, IV:42, IV:64,
IV:69–70, IV:84
one at a time, IV:86
open-ended, neutral, vs. closed or
leading, IV:83
setting-up, IV:84
quotations from interviews, use of,
III:110, V:109

R

recognition. *See* acknowledgements
recorder maintenance technicians, III:54
recording abstract, described, III:126
recording equipment
budgeting for, II:92
choosing, I:13, I:39–41, II:13, III:13,
III:83, IV:13, V:17
data capacity of, IV:62
development of digital, I:21
final check before interview of,
IV:61–62, IV:79–80
historical use of, I:20–21
kit contents, III:85–86
maintenance guidelines, III:87–88
management responsibilities, III:82,
III:86
maximum recordable time, IV:92
number of devices needed, IV:62
obtaining, III:84, III:98
post-interview tasks, IV:100

project director responsibilities, III:50
standards, II:119–23
storage space for, III:65
training workshops, III:88–90,
IV:52, IV:61–62
for transcribing, IV:106
troubleshooting problems, III:81–82
using free computer programs, III:84
using iPhones as, III:84
voice-activated, III:84
See also audio recording equipment;
microphones; video record-
ing equipment
*Recording Oral History: A Guide for the
Humanities and Social Sciences*
(Yow), I:22
recordings
long-term preservation, III:126–27,
III:128
post-interview tasks, III:133, V:50
recording technicians, III:53–54
record keeping
of all decisions made, II:44–46
ASAP post-interview, V:49–50
before-the-interview by interviewers, IV:72, IV:74
computer applications, V:39–40
as final processing step, V:54
master documents, V:40–41, V:105,
V:155n.3
overview of, II:66–67
planning for post-interview options,
II:99
post-interview by interviewers,
IV:98–100, IV:107–8
principles of good, V:40
of processing plan steps, V:37
review for all forms, V:24, V:26
review for all interviews, V:104
stages, V:50
systems compared, V:39, V:155n.4
technology decisions, I:42–43
timeliness in, V:40
training for interviewers, IV:53
See also cataloging; sample forms
reflection issues, V:107–8
Reid, Charissa, V:56
relational databases, V:81

remuneration policy, III:110
repositories
    acceptance of interviews having
        restrictions, V:28–29
    access and, III:132, III:133, V:93,
        V:156n.12
    accession numbers, V:41
    cataloging method and, V:74
    choosing, I:54–55, II:59–61,
        III:118–19, V:29–31
    collection of all items by interview-
        ers for, IV:108
    common guidelines of, II:61
    common questions from, II:62
    common questions to ask of, II:62
    confirmation with, V:26
    copyright and, IV:34, V:37, V:155n.2
    data files storage and maintenance
        by, III:85
    defining, II:58–59, V:22, V:29, V:99,
        V:156n.12
    digital, II:101, V:22, V:27, V:94–95
    historical societies as, II:102
    identifying at outset, I:37, I:46–47
    importance of, V:22–23
    Internet as, II:66
    Legal Release Agreements and,
        I:46–47, II:39
    Letter of Agreement for Repository,
        II:63–64, II:70–71, II:72
    libraries as, II:102, III:124
    master files and, V:105
    negotiating with, III:119
    overview of, III:118
    processing requirements of, III:111,
        III:125, V:27, V:52–54
    project director responsibilities,
        III:49
    technical requirements, I:46
    updating team and community
        about, III:49
    web-hosted, III:120, III:122
reproduction rights and copyright, II:37
research
    before-the-interview background,
        IV:40–42, IV:63–64
    identifying potential interviewees,
        IV:44–45

    on Internet, IV:41–42
    interviewee-specific, IV:64–65
    by interviewers, IV:28
    transcripts as tools for, V:57
    using during interviews, IV:90
researchers, handling inquiries from,
    V:108–9
resources, finding, I:36–37
reviews, as grant requirement, III:97
Ritchie, Don, V:91
Roadside Heritage, California project,
    V:126–28
Rocky Flats Cold War Museum project,
    I:56–57, III:129
Ross, Martha, IV:48, IV:55, IV:74

S
salvage oral history, defining, III:95
sample forms
    Cataloging Planning Chart, V:85–86
    Cataloging Protocol, I:75, I:84,
        V:86–87
    Cataloging Work Sheet, I:75, I:85,
        V:88–89
    Interviewee Biographical Profile,
        I:74, I:79, II:69, III:70–72,
        IV:66–67, V:44–45
    Interviewee Recommendation
        Form, I:74, I:78, II:68, III:69
    interview introduction, IV:68
    Interview Summary, I:74, I:80, II:70,
        III:73–74, IV:102–3, V:46–47
    Interview Tracking Form, I:74, I:82,
        II:71, III:75–76, V:48–49,
        V:155n.5
    Legal Release Agreement, I:75, I:86,
        II:40, III:44, IV:36, V:147–48
    Legal Release Agreement (Restric-
        tions), I:75–76, I:87, II:41,
        III:45, IV:37, V:149–50
    Letter of Agreement for Interviewer,
        I:76, I:89, II:72, III:60, IV:54
    Letter of Agreement for Repository,
        I:76, I:88, II:63, III:121, V:30
    Letter of Agreement for Transcriber,
        I:76, I:90, II:73, III:61, V:65
    letter to potential interviewee, IV:49
    management survey, III:139–47

Master Contact List, V:42
Photograph and Memorabilia
    Receipt, I:74, I:81, II:74,
    III:77–78, IV:99–100
Project Design Statement, I:74, I:77,
    II:45, V:135–46
Project Manual Table of Contents,
    V:106–7
templates, I:73
time sheets, III:62
Transcribing Guide, V:66–68
Transcription Protocol, I:75, I:83,
    V:60–61
scholarly research centers, I:20–21
school curriculum outcome example,
    V:122–23
scope of a project, II:50–52
scrapbooks, IV:42, IV:92
secondary sources
    defining, I:18
    primary sources vs., V:113, V:114
    See also outcomes
Shopes, Linda, V:120–21
slander issues, III:109, IV:31
Smith Club of Minnesota Oral History
    Project, II:97–98
social media, using wisely, IV:45
sociologists, oral historians compared to,
    I:26–27
solicited funds, II:96
Sommer, Barbara, V:121–23
sound, background, II:75
sound quality, maximizing, III:84
space needs
    for data files, II:79, II:81, II:92
    for interviews, II:75–76
    multiple sites, II:99
    for transcripts, V:55
    See also storage
spreadsheet record keeping system, V:39
stability
    commitment to project duration by
        team members, III:48, III:55
    importance of, III:49
stand alone collection management
    system, V:80–81
state funding sources, II:94

state humanities councils/historical soci-
    eties, as resource, I:37
static websites, V:102
storage
    costs of, II:59
    of data files, II:79, II:81, II:92,
        III:84–85
    of equipment, II:78, II:83
    libraries for, II:76
    multiple copies in different loca-
        tions, V:100
    offsite for documents, V:41
    questions to ask about, II:60
    security and accessibility of files,
        III:65, III:79
    space for audio vs. video files, III:85
    standards, II:123
StoryCorps, IV:22, IV:46, V:130
storytelling compared to oral history, I:17,
    I:25–26
subjectivity of historical record, I:19–20
subpoenas, III:110
support and funding. See funding; grants

T
talking head visuals, I:40
Tebeau, Mark, V:68–69
Tectonic Theater Project, V:123
telephone interviews, recording, I:42
templates. See sample forms
thank yous. See acknowledgements
theater outcome example, V:123–25
"They Changed the World: The People
    of Project Y at Los Alamos,
    1943–1945" (exhibit), V:128–30
Thucydides, I:20
time
    allocating, for transcribing, V:37
    average, for each interview, II:52,
        III:50, III:111
    commitment of team members,
        III:48, III:55, III:57–58
    requirements for processing,
        III:111–12, V:23, V:26
    sheets, III:62
    spent planning, III:18
time-coded indexes, V:69, V:126

Toolkit, overview of, I:11–13, I:67–71,
    II:11–13, III:11–13, IV:11–13,
    V:15–17
training
    addressing cross-cultural communi-
        cations during, IV:57
    to assure consistent quality, I:13,
        II:13, III:13, IV:13, V:17
    ethical dimensions of, IV:28
    importance of, I:34
    organizing and scheduling, III:50
    planning workshops, II:102–3
    for processing, V:26
    recording equipment workshops,
        III:88–90
    transcribers, II:102, III:50, III:130–32
    in use of recording technology, I:41
training of interviewers
    duration and attendance, II:102,
        IV:51–52
    on equipment use, IV:52, IV:61–62
    importance of, I:13, I:63, II:13, III:13,
        III:50, IV:13, IV:51, V:17
    topics to be covered, III:117–18,
        IV:52–53, IV:63
transcribers
    challenges for, I:48
    characteristics of good, III:53, V:58
    indexing by, IV:107
    interviewers as, IV:106
    Letter of Agreement sample, III:61,
        V:65
    Master Contact List of, V:42–43
    processing tasks, V:52
    pros and cons of roles, V:59
    responsibilities of, III:53, III:57
    training, II:102, III:50, III:130–32
    volunteers as, V:56
transcriber's packet
    contents of, V:64
    Letter of Agreement for Transcriber,
        V:65
    sample guide, V:66–68
transcribing
    allocating time for, V:37
    alternatives to, V:68–69

decisions about, IV:106
described, III:126
equipment, II:84, II:92, II:128n.16,
    IV:106
group interviews, IV:47
guide for, V:66–68
interviewers and, IV:106, IV:107
interview logs and, III:126
management tasks step-by-step,
    V:62–63
outsourcing, V:59
planning guide, II:100
processing steps, V:52
record keeping, V:60–62
steps, III:128–29
time needed per hour of interview
    for, III:111, V:26
Transcription Protocol, I:75, I:83, V:60–61
transcripts
    audio checking of, IV:107
    average number of pages, III:111–12
    contextual notes added, IV:30
    controlled vocabulary and, V:84
    defining, V:58
    described, III:126
    making multiple copies of, V:63
    pros and cons of, III:127, III:129,
        IV:106, V:55–57, V:68–69
    reading as theater performance,
        V:123
    repository and, V:37
    review by interviewees of, V:52, V:63
    sample excerpt, V:151–53
    verbatim, I:48–49
transparency, areas of, III:108
Twitter accounts, using wisely, IV:45
2008 election in Arapahoe County, Colo-
    rado project, I:29–30

U
University of California, I:20
University of Kentucky, I:52
Using Oral History in Community History
    Projects (Mercier and Buckend-
    orf), I:28, II:46–47, III:110

V

verbatim transcripts, I:48–49

video-conferencing technology, quality issues, I:42

videographers, training for, III:88–90

video media

delivery of, V:63

labeling, V:41–42

overview of post-interview tasks, V:50–51

as preservation format, V:96–97

time-coded indexes, V:69

transcribing from, V:62

video recording equipment

choosing, I:40–41, I:42, II:78–82, III:83

data format for, IV:62

ethical considerations, I:54

final check, IV:79–80

set-up at interview location of, IV:76–77

standards, II:120–21, II:122–23

video recording tips, IV:76–78

vocabulary

checking, IV:95

familiarity with unique project, IV:64

unfamiliar use of, by interviewee, IV:88

voice-activated equipment, III:84

Voice Preserve, V:95

volunteer fictitious project

advisory committees and, II:34

budget, II:93, III:103

cataloging of, II:101

catalog management system, V:80

management notes, III:30

overview of, II:23, II:24, III:20, III:30, V:80

processed interviews, III:111–12

Project Design Statement, III:31–33, V:135–38

team members, III:66

workflow planning, II:51

work space, III:67

volunteers

assessing need for additional, V:24

bibliography of known information for, IV:40, IV:42

budgeting as income, II:91, II:96

defining roles and values, II:96

documenting monetary value of, III:67, III:100–101

maintaining interest of, IV:32

Master Contact List of, V:42–43

permanent contact designée, V:104

recognizing contributions of, I:38

technology considerations and, I:41

as transcribers, V:56

typical number of interviews by, III:111

using successfully, I:33, I:34, III:63–64, IV:51

See also specific roles such as *interviewers*

W

walking tour outcome example, V:125–28

web-hosted repositories, III:120, III:122

websites

Densho Digital Archive, II:66

H-Oralhist, III:120

Maria Rogers Oral History Program, II:66

Minnesota Digital Library, II:66

Minnesota Historical Society, II:66

Montana Historical Society, II:66

Northeast Minnesota Historical Center, II:66

Oakland Chinatown Oral History Project, II:66

OHA, II:35, III:42, III:120

Roadside Heritage project, V:127–28

websites, using, III:133

budgeting for, III:102

defining, V:95

digital repositories and, V:22, V:27, V:94–95

dynamic/interactive, V:102

piggybacking onto existing, V:101–2

planning for, II:59, V:27

as repositories, V:22

static, V:102

YouTube as draw to, V:97

When the Levees Broke: a Requiem in Four Acts (film), V:115
Williamson, Mary Ann, V:116–18
Wiskemann, Geneva Kebler, III:25–26
Women in Journalism Oral History Project, IV:46
work space
    city fictitious project, III:67
    disposition of, at project end, V:104
    historical societies for, II:76
    historical society fictitious project, III:67
    interviewing area, II:75–76
    in libraries, II:76
    office area, II:76, V:38
    setting up, III:65
    volunteer fictitious project, III:67
Wyoming, Laramie Project, V:123

Y
Your Story and Mine: A Community of Hope (Advent House Ministries, Lansing, Michigan), 135–36
YouTube, V:97
Yow, Valerie Raleigh, I:22

Z
Zusman, Angela, V:105

ABOUT THE AUTHORS

Mary Kay Quinlan, Ph.D., is an associate professor at the University of Nebraska-Lincoln in the College of Journalism and Mass Communications. She has held positions at the University of Maryland, and has served as president of the National Press Club. She is editor of the Oral History Association Newsletter and co-author with Barbara Sommer of *The Oral History Manual*, 2nd ed. (AltaMira Press, 2009), *Native American Veterans Oral History Manual* (Nebraska Foundation for the Preservation of Oral History, 2005), and *Discovering Your Connections to History* (AASLH, 2000). She is also a co-author with Sommer and Charles E. Trimble of *The American Indian Oral History Manual: Making Many Voices Heard* (Left Coast Press, Inc., 2008).

Nancy MacKay, MLIS, has been straddling the line between libraries and oral history for more than twenty years. As a librarian she has worked with special collections, cataloging, and music in various academic settings. As an oral historian she teaches, consults, advises, and writes about oral history, especially oral history and archives. She directed the oral history program at Mills College, from 2001-2011, and currently teaches library science and oral history at San Jose State University. Nancy is the author of *Curating Oral Histories* (Left Coast Press, Inc., 2007).

Barbara W. Sommer, M.A., has more than thirty-five years' experience in the oral history field. She has been principal investigator and director of more than twenty major oral history projects and has taught at the University of Nebraska-Lincoln, Nebraska Wesleyan University, and Vermilion Community College, MN. She is author of many key publications in the field, including, with Mary Kay Quinlan, *The Oral History Manual*, 2nd ed. (AltaMira Press, 2009) and with Quinlan and Charles E. Trimble, *The American Indian Oral History Manual: Making Many Voices Heard* (Left Coast Press, Inc., 2008). Her award-winning book *Hard Work and a Good Deal: The Civilian Conservation Corps in Minnesota* (Minnesota Historical Society Press, 2008) draws on oral history interviews about the Civilian Conservation Corps.